DREAM WORLDS

Architecture and Entertainment

Text by Oliver Herwig
Photographs by Florian Holzherr

PRESTEL
MUNICH · BERLIN · LONDON · NEW YORK

For Henriette

© Prestel Verlag,
Munich · Berlin · London · New York 2006

Front and back cover: Las Vegas,
Nevada, USA
Front endpapers: WonderWorks, Orlando,
Florida, USA
pp. 4–5: Mall of America, Bloomington,
Minnesota, USA
pp. 6–7: Las Vegas, Nevada, USA
Back endpapers: Las Vegas, Nevada, USA

Prestel Verlag
Königinstrasse 9
80539 Munich
Tel. +49 (0)89-38 17 09-0
Fax +49 (0)89-38 17 09-35

Prestel Publishing Ltd.
4, Bloomsbury Place
London WC1A 2QA
Tel. +44 (0)20-73 23-5004
Fax +44 (0)20-76 36-8004

Prestel Publishing
900 Broadway, Suite 603
New York, NY 10003
Tel. +1 (212) 995-2720
Fax +1 (212) 995-2733

www.prestel.com

Library of Congress Control Number:
2006900789

British Library Cataloguing-in-Publication
Data: a catalogue record for this book is
available from the British Library

The Deutsche Bibliothek holds a record
of this publication in the Deutsche
Nationalbibliografie; detailed
bibliographical data can be found under
http://dnb.ddb.de

Translated from the German: Fiona Elliott, Edinburgh

Editorial direction: Sandra Leitte, Angeli Sachs
Copyediting: Jonathan Fox, Barcelona
Design, layout and production: René Güttler
Origination: Reproline Mediateam, Munich
Printing and binding: MKT Print d.d., Slovenia

Printed in Slovenia on acid-free paper

ISBN 3-7913-3220-1
978-3-7913-3220-8

Photo Credits

All photographs by Florian Holzherr, Munich, with the exception of: Archigram Archives, London: 25 ·
Maurice Bessy. *Charlie Chaplin*. London, 1985: 26 · Hervé Champollion: 24 · Cinetext, Frankfurt: 17 ·
www.emiratespalace.com: 146–149 · Engelhardt/Sellin: 39 · Gerhard Hagen/artur: 23 · Oliver Herwig: 72,
73, photo strips 42–134 · Herzog-August-Bibliothek, Wolfenbüttel: 14 · Bildagentur Huber: 70 · Werner
Huthmacher: 152 · IFA-Bilderteam: 56–57 · Courtesy The Jerde Partnership: 35 · LEGOLAND® Germany: 36 ·
Heiner Leiska: 33 · Nakheel Co LLC: 9 (7), 136–137, 144, 145 · Winfried Nerdinger and Kristiana Hartmann,
Matthias Schirren, Manfred Speidel, eds. *Bruno Taut. Architektur zwischen Tradition und Avantgarde.*
Stuttgart/Munich, 2001: 15 bottom left · Phoenix Resort, Ltd.: 138 · Stiftung Deutsche Kinemathek,
Berlin: 16 · Martin Thomas: 19 · Tropical Islands: 9 (6), 139, 142 · Virgilio Vercelloni. *Atlante storico
dell'idea europea della città ideale*. Milan, 1994: 15 bottom right · Volkswagen AG: 153

CONTENTS

WE DON'T GO FOR ENTERTAINMENT

Denise Scott Brown and Robert Venturi on Las Vegas

Have you been to Las Vegas lately?

Denise Scott Brown: Fairly recently ...
Robert Venturi: ... in the last few years we've been there a couple of times. We don't go for entertainment. I've never put one coin in a machine. I've never gambled. But we've learned from it.

And how did it feel?

RV: I must say we loved the earlier Las Vegas. And we don't love the current Las Vegas. We think it's right to analyze it and maybe we *should* love it and then we would learn from it.

Is Las Vegas now playing the duck-theme on a huge scale?

RV: That's a good way to put it. The earlier Las Vegas epitomized the decorated shed and the building itself was kind of neutral, loft-like, generic. The architecture now is sculptural, scenographic, symbolic.

What has changed exactly? Is it the perfection; the LED surfaces? Or the way Las Vegas pretends to be accessible while everything is private?

DSB: Everyone said there was nothing civic on the old Strip, no piazza, no place for civic life. But we pointed out there *was* a public sector— the street and sidewalks were public, and so were the street lights, traffic lights, and information signs. They were small but intense. There was an interesting play between the regularity of the light poles and traffic signs of the city and

10

the variety of buildings and signs of the private sector. But the private were controlled too, even though they seemed chaotic. They were well-organized functionally, and they were tuned to meet the geometry of the eye. The variety was under control, and both the variety and the control derived from the need to attract people in cars. This produced an almost mathematical order that was visible—if you knew how to look for it. The public control was less visible but it was there, even if people thought there was nothing public in Las Vegas.

RV: The highway was.

DSB: The highway and the sidewalk. Now the Strip is called Las Vegas Boulevard and it's full of plazas. They *look* public but they're private. Even the sidewalk is private. If you want to demonstrate on the Las Vegas Boulevard sidewalks, you might think you're allowed because you're in the public sector, but all that remains public is 18 inches of curb on the street. The

rest of the sidewalk belongs to the property owners and you can't do anything there that they disapprove of.

Is the old Las Vegas, the one you analyzed, irrelevant now?

DSB: The Las Vegas we talked about is historical now but we think it's still relevant. The new Las Vegas is essentially a theme park, a Disneyland, the city as scenography.

RV: I don't think it's all that new. The Italians were pretending they were Romans when they built in Florence and elsewhere during the Renaissance. So, the idea of architecture as symbolic background and the city as scenography has precedents, and architects who are examining the new Las Vegas, updating our studies 25 years later, are continuing to learn from it. But do they love it?

PARADISE LOST
In Search of Utopia

The Fountain of Youth, the Land of Milk and Honey, El Dorado, Shangri-la, Xanadu — the dream of a life of ease and plenty has many names. One constant in all these fantasies is their striking physicality, as in the Land of Cockaigne, that medieval home to laggards and gluttons with its streets of ginger, its sausage trees, and its roast doves that fly into one's mouth. Mountains of gruel demand to be physically overcome by those wishing to enter this land. What a nightmare for societies of choles-

terol-conscious, workout enthusiasts! Evidently, the dreams of those living in developed countries have changed dramatically. No longer do we suffer from a lack of food, rather a lack of exercise is our bane. A highly sophisticated leisure industry has created a world of fast-food chains and standardized leisure pursuits perfected over the course of the last one hundred years. Vacations and free time are professionally organized, and because time is short, everything has to be just right: fun according to a plan. Dream worlds are

Pieter Bruegel the Elder, The Land of Cockaigne, 1567, Alte Pinakothek, Munich, Germany

Vision of Atlantis based on Plato's description

incarnations of our fun society, modern places of pilgrimage providing the same kind of overwhelming experience that was once only to be had in the grand cathedrals. As commercial counterparts to the latter, they celebrate transient pleasures: *carpe diem* on a hitherto unknown scale. Dream worlds earn billions — an astounding phenomenon — demonstrating how pleasure can become a brand: precisely defined, standardized, quality-controlled, and available on demand. Las Vegas and Orlando have perfected the art of the themed experience and have, in the process, set the gold standard in the leisure industry, known to all, and there for any would-be competitor to measure up to. So come with us on five expeditions to distraction and diversion, to mega-malls and theme parks, artificial tropical paradises, and aging amusement parks, on a journey to uncover the sediments of popular culture: garish, brash, and glittering. And what you see here is what matters, for as Josef Albers once said, appearances are the only things that do not deceive.

In Search of Utopia

Since time immemorial the human race has been searching for its lost paradise, only to move ever further from it as civilization progresses — a productive paradox, like Utopia itself, that nonplace, that one can neither enter nor occupy yet which has been such a spur to architects' imaginations. Three great narratives have fed the Western hemisphere's fantasies of ideal cities: Plato's account of the city of Atlantis in his *Timaeus* and *Critias* dialogues; the vision of a heavenly Jerusalem in the Bible; and Thomas More's *Utopia*. The ideal society constructs for itself a geometric ideal city, either laid out in concentric circles or as a perfect square. Internal order is reflected in the visible layout. The island kingdom of Atlantis (approximately 11,500 BC) embodies the Pythagorean cosmos. Ten spheres of concentric channels and walls surround a pillar inscribed with the laws of the land. A sun-like center point, together with the temple of the god of the sea and a sacred grove, demonstrate the symbolic union of divine and human order in the laws. The walls denote the value of what they are protecting: the outermost wall is of stone, the wall around the grove is made from orichalcum, and the royal palace is surrounded by gold.

Plato laid out his city without regard for topography; the radiant, heavenly city of Jerusalem, described in the Book of Revelations and filled with the glory of God, is beyond both

The Heavenly Jerusalem, gleaming with twelve precious stones, Herzog-August-Bibliothek, Wolfenbüttel, Germany

time and place. As a vision of the end of time, it supersedes Babylon. While Babylon is the epitome of destruction, the heavenly Jerusalem embodies perfection. A square city wall with twelve Gates on which are written the names of the tribes of the Children of Israel surrounds the Lord's throne, which replaces the temple. Materials signal that this is the final act of creation: the foundation stones are precious stones; each gate is a pearl; the streets are made of gold. And the river of the Water of Life proceeds from God's throne, with the Tree of Life on either side of it — promising the ultimate paradise.

Thomas More's *Utopia* of 1516, on the other hand, describes a perfect earthly nation-state on a peninsula originally named Abraxa which, on Utopus' orders, was turned into a crescent-shaped, unassailable, artificial island separated from the mainland by a specially-dug channel, fifteen-miles-long. On the island itself there are fifty-four large, well-built cities distributed evenly across the territory. The capital is Amaurot. All the cities are laid out according to the same plan: "If you know one of their cities you know them all."[1] The square capital city is divided into four equal districts with a market in the center of each. Town planning here is nothing short of perfection. The streets are designed not only for vehicles and transportation but also to provide protection from the wind. The three-story houses are built from "fieldstone," with flat, fireproof, plaster-covered roofs. They have gardens so that the occupants can provide for themselves, and every ten years the houses change hands. There is no such thing as private property here, though, from a present-day point of view, this is where the advantages end. Society in Utopia is a patriarchal gerontocracy. The elders are elected to the highest positions; decisions are reached in the senate, which also keeps the princes in check. Public safety is one part of the social contract; service to one's fellow citizens is another. Every two years the townspeople and the country folk exchange roles, and since everyone without exception is gainfully employed, a six-hour working day provides the people with more than enough. There is no need for private possessions, for "the chief aim of their constitution is that all citizens should be free to withdraw as much time as possible from the service of the body and devote themselves to the freedom and culture of the mind. For in that, they think, lies the happiness of life."[2]

In his two-part work, More established a new genre, a literary riposte to the existing social order. The places he describes were never more than a fiction. Even the ideal cities of the past could not match up to Utopia.[3] In any age, they merely reflect contemporary ideals of social interaction, which are then embodied in the planning. Utopia as a genre has nothing to do with this. There is a clear division in the spectrum of Utopias: works that see history as moral decay and decadence, prototypical descriptions of an imagined Golden Age, projections of a perfect future, and others posited on wholesale destruction—dystopias. Utopias put forward ideas and concepts that pre-empt the conflicts that first erupted in the twentieth and twenty-first centuries. Utopia ⸱⸱⸱ies represent the typical notion of a perfect society. The square and the circle are superhuman in their perfection. In reality, architects and builders have no choice but to proceed in the opposite direction. In the absence of an ideal society, they turn their attention to the shell, the city itself, as an ideal form. And in the twentieth century, this is increasingly replaced by themed environments, arcades, mega-malls, and amusement parks.

Welcome to the Pleasure Dome!

The notion of gods as jaded immortals is a familiar one. Not so the idea that they use mortals — their creations — to stave off their boredom. Zeus plays with them, tests them, delights in their battles, and yet is nothing more than a projection of their own wishes and longings. But what if the gods' creations become all-powerful and hence immortal, too? What happens when technology replaces nature? "Anything to relieve the boredom!" moans one of the chosen ones in the sci-fi movie *Zardoz*; he wants to break out of the artificially contented community of immortals — phlegmatic and overcome by boundless lethargy — who languish in a society without excitement or goals: "They're all dead! Died of boredom."

This elite community, which has overcome death, longs for it all to end but its members are not able to escape from their perfect, static world where time stands still. "We're trapped by our own devices. There's no exit," cry the Immortals who have yielded to technology and have enslaved the world around them. A Brutal has to come from the world beyond this idyll in order to destroy it. He stinks, he is uncouth, but he is their last hope of tricking their way out of the dream world and once again taking their place in the natural cycle of life.

In the past, dream worlds were meant to liberate human beings from the whims of nature; nowadays they are more about escaping our work-oriented society. In mega-malls, in Disneyland and Las Vegas there is neither hunger nor suffering nor death. The idyll is utterly artificial and consists of optical illusions with the producer and user happily exchanging knowing glances. It is made of sets constructed from steel and glass, papier maché and paint. Where the existing technology is not sufficient, it is the role of the illusion to temporarily liberate the customer from their daily rounds. No country does this with such supreme mastery as the United States of America, which long ago established the pursuit of happiness as an inviolable right — be it in the real world or in a digital scenario, in the national

Bird's eye view of Bruno Taut's ideal city, The City Crown, 1919

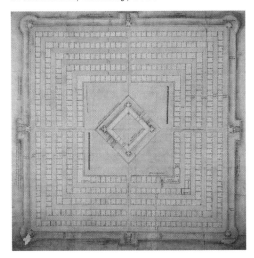

Plan for an ideal city by Heinrich Schickhardt, Freudenstadt, Germany, 1599

parks as the precursors to the theme park, creating an illusion of natural surroundings and untouched nature; or in the gaming worlds constructed on the Russian doll principle: the town in the town in the world, as at Disney.

Checklist for Dream Worlds

Dream worlds are ...

... all about scale. It is not by chance that they are called "lands" or "worlds." Children tend to attach great importance to small things and to sink into their own fantasy worlds; adults, who have largely lost this capacity, withdraw into the world of hobbies, model railroads, and gardening. Small things acquire a new importance, as does one's time out from the workaday world. And this is where the professional dream-world providers step in. In their hands, the dream reigns supreme and they promise us total immersion, utterly detached from our everyday lives.

... all about detachment. Dream worlds thrive on the exclusion of the many for the sake of the exclusive community of the few. Walls and boundaries reflect the appeal of what is contained within. Disneyland is still shielded by embankments like Cockaigne behind its mountains of gruel. Disney World, on the other hand, situated within a huge private estate with ample room for another half-dozen amusement parks, manages without, although the ticket booths and the entrance gates will never disappear.

... all about technology. Dream worlds have always striven for the very latest in technological advances. They work with strong stimuli. Convincing sets and decor are good; hyperrealism is better. Dream worlds rely heavily on the latest media, a perfect screenplay, and the right sets. The stuff that dreams are made of has changed, it has dematerialized like stage directions. Once upon a time sets were made from papier maché, plywood, and paint; but now, digital simulations — bits and bytes that

Erich Kettelhut's scenery for the film "Metropolis" by Fritz Lang, 1927

Virtual scenery from the film "Sin City", 2005

produce living images—stimulate visitors' imaginations.

... a commercially optimized mass product. Dream worlds are hierarchical structures; they realize and apply ideas top-down and according to strict time lines. They represent an ideal order. Reality is spontaneous, chaotic, and parallel; dream worlds are, by contrast, controlled and sequential, a precisely planned route without detours or shortcuts, so the visitor can be sure of replicating that same experience as often as they like, in the spirit of the notion that happiness is nothing other than the desire for repetition. Satisfaction guaranteed.

... a reflection of our society, its desires and fantasies. As such, they are not utopias, but play their part in the search for meaning. Dream worlds are not about ethics, and certainly not about morals, although this is not to say that they have no standards—on the contrary. Rarely is the principle of *laissez faire* rendered as inoperative as in dream worlds, which cleanly and rigorously exclude anything in the least bit disturbing—even their visitors' fantasies, if they happen not to be in keeping with the product.

1 Thomas More, *Utopia*, ed. George M. Logan and Robert M. Adams, Cambridge Texts in the History of Political Thought (Cambridge, UK, 2003), p. 44.
2 Ibid., p. 53.
3 The history of the ideal city and of utopian literature is well described by Ruth Eaton, *Ideal cities: Utopianism and the (Un)Built Environment* (London, 2002) and by Karl R. Kegler, Karsten Ley, and Anke Naujokat, *Utopische Orte: Utopien in Architektur- und Stadtbaugeschichte* (Aachen, 2004), p. 18.

PRE-FABRICATED DREAMS

Architecture for Pleasure

Panem et circenses—Juvenal's pithy comment on the passions of the Roman proletariat who, *en masse*, streamed to the banks of the Tiber from all over the Empire: ample food and spectacular entertainment to keep unrest at bay. Equestrian games, gladiatorial combat, and animal baiting went on for days on end; eager spectators would crowd into the arenas at night to secure the best seats for the next day. For the Romans, these games were a way of paying tribute to their gods, and they were attended by even the most noble dignitaries who otherwise resided in grand villas outside the city. Rome, with a population of over one million, had a problem: in the third century AD around 15 percent of the population was provided for by the state. On feast days—182 in total—the masses could attend free events in the Colosseum, with seating for around 100,000, or in the much larger Circus Maximus. This huge building, 361 feet wide and 2,083 feet long (110 x 635 m)—which took generations for the city's imperial rulers to construct—could ultimately accommodate up to 385,000 baying Romans.[1] On one side of this elongated oval were the *carceres* with twelve double doors, which would suddenly fly open as the chariots shot out onto the track. The charioteers had to survive seven laps around the arena, approximately 5.5 miles (8.5 km). At the end of each lap, a silver dolphin or a marble egg would be removed under the gaze of the masses feverishly anticipating the end of the race. Rowdies, chants, and fan clubs—the strictly organized racing corporations had it all. The masses supported the Whites, Reds, Greens, or Blues; in 532 AD, the feud between the Greens and the Blues escalated into a bloodthirsty civil war in Constantinople, the capital of the Eastern Roman Empire. Public spectacles became ever more ambitious. Emperor Claudius, for one, put on a *naumachia* (a lake drama) at Lake Fucino with a cast of 19,000—an army devoted to the people's entertainment; the celebrations to mark Trajan's victorious campaign in Dacia in 109 AD lasted 117 days. The bloody toll of these organized mass murders: 9,824 gladiators left the sandy arena as winners (victor), as pardoned men (missus), or as corpses (mortuus). Professional gladiators were idolized and earned huge sums until Emperor Honorius banned the *munera gladiatoria* in 404 AD.

What Torrents of Water!

Mass entertainment needs a monumental setting. On the terraces, all men are equal. "From early on in the morning, one sees the most elegant toilettes fighting over seats with the wildest looking Abruzzi," to quote Stendhal in his description of the love of spectacle that united the various levels of Roman society. "As soon as the peasant has just two carlin in his pocket, he sits himself down next to the Roman Principe. In this place of equality money creates the only recognized and privileged aristocracy."[2] Architecture becomes part of the scene, providing a stunning backdrop. The ancient builders and architects set new standards with the Circus Maximus, the Arena in Verona, the Hippodrome, and the Theater at Epidauros. The Colosseum—still impressive

The Colosseum, Rome, Italy, begun in 72 AD, opened in 80 AD

today, even as a two thousand-year-old ruin—is a virtuosic combination of dramatic design and logistics, with around 87,000 seats and standing room for a further 15,000 to gaze in rapt attention at sea battles, animal baiting, and gladiatorial combat. For the inauguration of the Colosseum in 80 AD, five thousand animals were slaughtered and the celebrations lasted for a hundred days. Rome, the nerve center of the known world, sucked the provinces dry. The metropolis and its mob had to be fed and watered, to the tune of a billion cubic meters of water per day, which poured into the wells and thermal baths from thirteen aqueducts. Throughout the Empire, wherever there were amphitheaters it was the citizens' right to relax and forget about the not-so-happy *dolce far niente*. At the thermal baths—the high-tech architecture of antiquity—in spite of moments of reconciliation, two very different worlds are in evidence: mass entertainment on one hand and the luxurious existence of the very few on the other. "What throngs of statues, what crowds of columns which, bearing nothing,

merely stand there as decoration, for the sake of embellishment! What torrents of water tumbling noisily down the steps," was Seneca's comment on the love of grandeur in his own day, after a visit to the villa of Scipio the Elder. In the end, it was only the French Revolution and the incipient media age that took the shine off the favorite haunts of the leisure classes. Pavilions, fantasy castles, tea houses, and follies in extensive parklands now became generally accessible—as public gardens and secularized grandeur—or at least accessible via the new media, without, as it happens, having to forfeit any of their function as catalysts of wishful bourgeois thinking. To this day entertainment architecture is poised on the dividing line between the mass market and exclusive retreats, which serve as reservoirs for other dreams. Conspicuous consumption is largely accepted when the stars of the tabloids—modern-day gladiators—live up to their roles as figures to be identified with, and leave the door to jet-set living slightly ajar.

Attractions, Attractions!

Since the mid-nineteenth century, the spectrum of entertainment architecture has been enriched by the advent of three new genres: world expositions, department stores, and amusement parks. For their part, these three genres express different social currents which—reinforcing each other in turn—culminated in modernism: paid labor and mass production, a working-class proletariat, the technology of the new media, and the aggressive modes of presentation preferred by increasingly global industries which used world expositions as showcases for their latest products. These expositions became "places of pilgrimage to the commodity fetish,"[3] as Walter Benjamin wrote in his unfinished *Arcades Project*; in his view, industry, apparently providing entertainment for the working classes, was only out to capture more customers. The carefully staged setting transfigured the exchange value of the goods and, as Benjamin said, the world expositions opened up "a phantasmagoria which a person enters in order to be distracted."[4]

Benjamin's "enthroning of goods" aimed to achieve increasingly extravagant modes of presentation and exhibition design. New materials—glass, iron, and steel—and electric lighting made them gleam; they appeared limpid, fluid, almost immaterial. Exhibition premises such as the Palais de l'Electricité at the 1900 World Exposition in Paris were no longer buildings as such, but manifestos, celebrating the marvels of electricity and artificial lighting. The continually contracting world was unrelentingly lauded in increasingly new, exotic modes of presentation at the same time as it was being reduced to a simple formula, which the travel business gladly latched onto later. Whereas since 1851 world expositions have been primarily a shop window for the different industrialized host nations, a carefully calculated input of exoticism—Indian palaces, Arabian bazaars—became a permanent fixture of their presentation methods. Added to which, the expositions were seen as an excuse to embark on spectacular building projects that used new materials—iron and glass for London's Crystal Palace in 1851; iron for the Eiffel Tower in 1889, which

Le Palais de l'Electricité, Expo 1900, Paris, France

The Father of Exhibition Venues: London's Crystal Palace, designed by Joseph Paxton, opened in 1851

was to be the tallest structure in the world for half a century—bold construction methods, and technical innovations on a scale previously unknown. The structures designed to house the world expositions stood as national symbols and increasingly defined European capitals. Revolutionary architectural designs became sources of wonder, exhibition pieces in their own right, an amalgam of engineering, excitement, and spectacular forms. The Eiffel Tower established iron as a building material once and for all; almost seventy years later the Brussels Atomium became the symbol of the new nuclear age.

The rise in consumerism led to the development of new exhibition spaces: roofed shopping arcades, where customers were protected from the weather, and department stores turned Paris into the leading metropolis of the nineteenth century. Almost one hundred and fifty years later Jon Jerde was to show that his malls are in no sense merely enlarged copies of the "arcades" developed in Paris and perfected in Milan; his designs are autonomous worlds that have no need of a context in order to function.

And then there was a third element: the amusement park, which combined the bourgeois, eighteenth-century public gardens—still steeped in the spirit of the nobility, where ladies with parasols and gentlemen in coattails would stroll at their leisure—with the somewhat dubious world of the fairground carnival, booths, and the circus ring. The earlier pleasure grounds with their artificial ruins, grottos and follies, exotic garden architecture, and water features were suddenly confronted with new inventions—steel-built attractions such as Ferris wheels, music halls, and oversized sculptures. Following the establishment of the privately-run Vauxhall Gardens in London, the Tivoli Park, constructed in Copenhagen in 1843, was the first park designed entirely around a single theme and became the model for similar parks in Europe and the United States. Street cafés, music halls, circus shows—the cities pulsated with life and a new popular culture emerged, offering the consumer spectacles of every possible kind. As far back as the eighteenth century, equestrian displays had already been captivating audiences.

The nineteenth century delighted in luxurious, glass-roofed arcades like the Galleria Vittorio Emanuele II, built in Milan between 1865 and 1867.

In the mid-nineteenth century, these were followed by circus shows in purpose-built circular structures such as the Cirque Napoléon of 1852, with a cantilevered auditorium measuring 131 feet (40 m) in diameter. The spectators were seated right next to the ring as if they were directly involved in the performance, until the turn of the century and the arrival of much larger circus buildings with seating for vast numbers.

One City—One Amusement Park

In the early twentieth century, almost every city had its own amusement park. Writers articulated the changing perception brought about by the electrification of public gardens. Stefan Zweig found himself "magically attracted" to the Prater in Vienna, and felt an affinity with "the animal nature" of what he saw there, its "instinctiveness" and "baseness."[5] In a similar vein, Ernst Bloch saw the amusement park as a fantastic

dream world, a subtly vulgar borderland.[6] While architecture matched these developments by becoming banal, decorative, and gaily abandoned, fairs and carnivals, all operated according to the same principle: life as a never-ending land of milk and honey, a sensual sensation which—like the Carnival in Venice—in fact helped to stabilize society. After the riotous fun, respectability and order were quickly restored. And it is interesting to observe the sensations that the masses craved: speed and bright lights, which were amply supplied by the new Ferris wheels and big dippers, and the thrill of losing control. Roller coasters today give customers butterflies in their stomachs but also appeal to their aesthetic sense. What are they if not monumental sculptures, the only spatial works of art developed in the twentieth century that people joyfully relish? They glorify the mobility of a society that has signed up to excessive speed and motion, to the extent that in Japan, where earthquakes are a constant danger, people take a particular delight experiencing the consequences of the Earth's movements in ultra-realistic disaster movies. When the skyscrapers sway and civilization collapses, the movie releases cathartic energies and becomes a fetish that wards off the forces of destruction for a brief period of heart-stopping entertainment.

The search for the ultimate thrill is not just about technical extremes of height and speed. It is also about fantastic journeys. There is only one limitation—the human being. When twenty-eight passengers on the Eurostar roller coaster swing into a curve, huge forces are exerted on the undercarriage: a horizontal load of thirty tons, equivalent to around twenty medium-sized automobiles. In addition to this, the passengers are pressed into their molded seats by five times their own body weight, like an Apollo astronaut during liftoff. Werner Stengel, an engineer with a passion for tight curves, has designed over two hundred roller coasters worldwide. Without his "heart line," which locates the carriage's center of gravity and pivot at chest height, the modern loops—"corkscrews" and "inverted coasters"— would be unthinkable. The steel tracks bank outward so that the passengers travel on more subtle curves such that jarred spines and neck injuries have become a thing of the past. At Cedar Point in the United States, passengers plunge downwards from a steely mountainside; Millennium Force, where only superlatives apply, accelerates to a speed of 93 miles (150 km) per hour, so that the passengers then find themselves gliding—weightless—over the so-called camel's back, undulations in the track that cause the passengers to rise minimally out of their seats giving them the feeling of floating—air time—until the eddy-current brake returns everyone to reality again.

The unstoppable rise of the entertainment industry has not been greeted with universal approval. Collective dreams have turned into fast food idylls; the particular is ousted by chains and clichés. And Wilhelm Genazino, with an eye to Adorno's critique of totalitarian entertainment, sees the masses as no different from the baying Romans: "Reinforcing their political malleability—of which those swept along by the latest entertainment should remain unaware—the culture industry works at creating an all-embracing, all-pervasive state of mind. And the prize for this submission—which is at the root of the enthusiasm of the masses—is the temporary banishment of the sense of emptiness that affects all layers of society."[7] Evidently, we have never moved from our seats on the terraces of the Colosseum, however much time has passed.

The Ancients' pleasure in arenas and thermal baths—which grew increasingly grandiose as those who financed them vied with each other for public appointments—is still part of life today. The only difference is that the plebeians seeking distraction in public games from the bleak hopelessness of their daily lives have now been replaced by hard-working men and women indulging themselves a little after the office has closed, and politically ambitious entrepreneurs such as Crassus, Pompey, and Caesar have been replaced by the leisure industry which channels collective dreams—sun, sand, and palms—into mass-consumable products. Anyone out to kill time these days no longer seeks out some blood-thirsty spectacle, but goes instead to the multiplex or boards an airplane.

Herzog & de Meuron, Allianz Arena, Munich, Germany, 2002–05

Polyclitus the Younger, Theater of Epidaurus, c. 400 BC

Fast Food Fantasy

Society today is all about having fun, says Neil Postman. And when we kill ourselves laughing, it's the most fun—as it is for the corporations running the gigantic amusement parks, who watch their coffers swell. Today, the standards for mass-entertainment are set in the United States, by Hollywood and Walt Disney. And the formula for guaranteed family fun has been found in the Disney theme parks—Disneyland in Anaheim, California, Disney World in Orlando, Florida, and Disneyland Resort near Paris. A whole industry is trying to emulate them, as entertainment has become a multibillion-dollar business.[8] And even if experiment and constant change have a part in this, there is no need to search for new formulas. The marketplace determines what is possible and the buyers go for what has already been tried and tested. Just as the steak metamorphosed into the hamburger sold at stalls at Coney Island and has now become the staple of the fast-food industry, entertainment today also has to be about success. Disneyland is not as profitable as it because of

constant innovation, but on the contrary, because it gives consumers what they already know. Again and again, guaranteed: fast-food dreams in fantasy worlds and in architectural settings palatable to the masses. Architainment, combining architecture and entertainment, is about ready-made, mass-consumable dreams—from the Circus Maximus to the sports arena, from the World Exposition to Expo and from Greek theatre to the Pleasure Dome. There are certain constants in the history of the architecture of entertainment, and one major change: our own media age has replaced matter with information and space with time. Architecture becomes a label and a backdrop, quotable and stackable, emotionalized and standardized. The precursor and master of this development is Las Vegas, a postmodern milestone of sampled and labeled facades: a *mise-en-scène* of temporary escape. Sets, screens, and the use of modern media are the hallmarks of modern dream worlds. Their hardware is nothing without the right software. Architecture becomes an interchangeable backdrop onto which are projected themes from Hollywood, our modern

Archigram, Plug-In City, aerial view, 1964–66

myths. Whole theme-towns are conjured up. Global playgrounds—the corollary of the service society with its vast leisure-time potential and thirst for adventure—become increasingly sophisticated in their scenarios, aiming to satisfy every taste. The small moment of happiness becomes part of a great narrative that is universally understood. Marketing strategies promoting adventure converge with narrative strategies developed in Hollywood. We want to be deceived, but with a money-back guarantee. Architecture becomes the, the fashionably styled backdrop, which has a precisely calculated half-life, as long as it is deemed fit as a setting and projection surface for our collective desires. In the hands of the entertainment industry, dream worlds become the stuff of a universal marketing strategy. Their architecture is influenced by studio sets, cites historical buildings, and takes what it wants from that legacy of the 1960s, Archigram, with its inspired combination of amusement and architecture. Distraction—once used to satiate the Roman masses, later the preserve of the privileged few—is on offer once again: at football

grounds, in Olympic stadiums, and in the giant hotels and beach clubs at more or less exotic holiday destinations. It is everywhere and with much the same standards. No one can escape the entertainment market these days.

1 The figures vary considerably. In the literature, they range from 190,000 to twice this number.
2 Stendhal, *Rome, Naples and Florence* (London 1959).
3 Walter Benjamin, *The Arcades Project*, ed. Roy Tiedemann, trans. Howard Eiland and Kevin McLaughlin (Cambridge MA, 1999), p. 7.
4 Ibid.
5 Regina Dahmen-Inghoven, *Animation—Form follows Fun* (Basel, 2004), p. 145.
6 Ernst Bloch, *The Principle of Hope* (Cambridge MA, 1996).
7 Wilhelm Genazino, "Der Professor im Schrank: Adorno und die Verweigerung des Lachens," in idem, *Der gedehnte Blick* (Munich, 2004):170–90, pp. 172–3.
8 Theme park attendance grew 3% during 2000 to reach a historic 175.1 million visitors, according to *Amusement Business* magazine. See: http://www.yesterland.com/parklinks.html.

IDEAL CITIES
Their Rise and Fall in the 20th Century

"Utopia is tomorrow's reality,"[1] announced Le Corbusier, and he started to draw. Like Georges-Eugène Haussmann in the mid-nineteenth century—who cut long, straight lines into the medieval city of Paris, boulevards that "collect together the little streets like great rivers absorbing their tributaries"[2]—Le Corbusier dismissed traditional concepts with a geometric mega-structure that could be replicated anywhere and at any time: crystalline rigor, perfect aesthetics, a "game of pure geometric consequences."[3] With the advent of modernism, the possibilities open to town planners multiplied. Having broken down the castle walls in the nineteenth century, a once static society now discovered what it was to become mobile; circulation and currents now shaped the picture of the city which grew into a metropolis. In the maelstrom of flowing monies, goods, and peoples, utopian and rational town planning eddied and swirled around each other. In the name of progress, architects emerged as the creators of new societies. Delusions of omnipotence were rife. Claude Nicolas Ledoux famously summed up the noblest tasks of the architect: "Everything comes under his aegis—politics, morals, jurisdiction, culture, government."[4] The ideal modernist city tapped into the energies and images of the machine age. Antonio Sant'Elia adorned his Città Nuova (1914) with monuments to movement: every design an airport or a station, every sketch a picture of movement with a monorail or elevator; metaphors of modernity that have no need of human operators, as

though in anticipation of the mechanized horrors of the First World War with its trenches and its "storms of steel" that saw the dreams of a whole generation perish.

Dynamite Flung into the Streets!

More enticing than Sant'Elia's heroic city is the sound of Taylor's ideal city. Its rhythms are set by functionality, perfection is its goal. The individual human being, conditioned to make just a few movements, becomes part of an impenetrable

Charlie Chaplin in "Modern Times", 1936

Antonio Sant'Elia, La Città Nuova, 1914

mechanism of the kind Charlie Chaplin so masterfully envisioned in his film *Modern Times* (1936). Urban hygiene becomes one of the watchwords of the time, with the result that rationally planned schemes for the masses were designed in a correspondingly sterile manner. Forty years later Ludwig Hilberseimer admitted that his 1924 high-rise city was simply a sea of asphalt and cement, more like a necropolis than a metropolis.[5] But Hilberseimer was not alone, and it was not only the Futurists who welcomed the new as death to the organic city, the rationalists were similarly keen to dispense with the organic city. The overarching plan now found favor. Le Corbusier replaced the nooks and crannies of history with a grid of arteries designed to accommodate the exponential increase in vehicular traffic, which he wanted to order and channel onto different levels. Wild,

undifferentiated currents—"dynamite flung into the streets"[6]—are disentangled and controlled. *Une ville contemporaine* was the name Le Corbusier gave to his 1922 design for a city of three million. At the drawing board, he created the apotheosis of rational transportation routes, which meet at the heart of a district with mega high-rise buildings and terraced homes. Purely provocative! And a miscalculation, which meant that henceforth Le Corbusier would suit his ubiquitous universal city to a specific location. Three years later he came up with his Plan Voisin (1925), which proposed to implant in Paris star-shaped, high-rise buildings like a new heart. Immediately next to the Louvre are eighteen mega-towers enclosing a rectangle where the metro (underground), the railway (overland) and air lines (above ground) all come together, forming the basis for a wholly modern city, an ideal city dedicated to movement and travel. The cruciform skyscrapers look like a phalanx of frozen propellers on a gigantic piece of machinery heading off into the future, a snapshot that captures the energy of pent-up movement. Le Corbusier sought provocation; he was out to attack the very core of Western urbanism, which held the human being as the yardstick for its planning processes, rather than the car or the airplane. It was not until American town planners and architects, such as Victor Gruen, came onto the scene with their motorized view of society that buildings were first designed to withstand extreme speeds; buildings that also parried the motion of the viewers with reduced facades, buildings that had become signs. Europe, on the other hand, capitulated in 1925 to Le Corbusier's radical plan for a city of movement, to be financed by the aeronautical engineer Voisin. "A city made for speed is a city made for success,"[7] to quote one of Le Corbusier's slogans for his Plan Voisin, which Kenneth Frampton discusses with cutting irony: "… rhetoric … accompanied his 'Plan Voisin' … —the paradoxical notion that the automobile having effectively destroyed the great city could now be exploited as an instrument for its salvation."[8]

With a single stroke of his pen, Le Corbusier had decided the center/periphery issue. The central park is a much-used hub, and the absolute periphery, so to speak. What the palace and the temple are to Plato, Thomas More, and the Bible—the core of the community, to which everything relates and which makes sense of things, became an interface in his plan: after almost two thousand years of urban construction, the cross became a crossing. The centrifugal forces of modernity broke new ground. Haussmann's hope of countering revolutionary Paris with the trajectories of his boulevards looks like an anachronism compared to the streets liberated by their own residents, which now only serve as lines connecting two points.

Metropolis Without a Center

After the failure of Le Corbusier's provocative proposals for Paris, the metropolis—with different districts for living and working—at the very least, became the model for CIAM and the Charter of Athens (1943), and influenced the thinking of an entire generation of town planners. Whole series of cities were built according to the Le Corbusier model. At the same time, the 1939 New York World's Fair—with Norman Bel Geddes's *Futurama* and Henry Dreyfuss's *Democracity*—promoted the decentralized, pluralistic metropolis of the automobile, in a sense developing Frank Lloyd Wright's Broadacre City (1934–35), a metropolis without a center or urban crowding and which seeks to do all of its functions equal justice in the expanses of the American landscape. The town/country dichotomy —which More wanted to solve by regularly swapping the different populations, and Edward Bellamy in his bestseller *Looking Backward: 2000–1887* (written in 1888) wanted to resolve in a socialist urban future—became all the more acute in the twentieth century. While the garden city movement, led by Ebenezer Howard, sought to reconcile the two poles in an egalitarian society, the pendulum ultimately swung towards a global urbanization that affects increasing numbers of people. In view of the expanding number of mega-cities and the evident inability of modern (Western) urban planning to cope with the chaotic growth of the metropolis, the ideal city movement lost its impetus, albeit not without having first inspired a small number of projects that won worldwide recognition. Significantly, these ideal cities emerged in the so-called Third World in the form of Chandigarh (1951–65) and Brasilia (1957–60); administrative centers which grew out of nothing and whose drawing board designs were soon overtaken and reshaped by the realities of daily life. They so physically embodied the progress of mobility that, in the case of Brasilia, the city itself took on the shape of a gigantic bird, coming in to land on the Distrito Federal. Or taking off, depending on how one sees it. Lucio Costa's 1957 design separates

Norman Bel Geddes' Futurama at the 1939 New York World's Fair

Paris buried under a grid of high-rise blocks. Le Corbusier's 1925 Plan Voisin was the apotheosis of the mobile, modernist city.

Frank Lloyd Wright, Broadacre City, project, 1934–35

traffic according to speed: expressways form the primary network for private vehicles, with subsidiary streets branching off at regular intervals into the various districts of the city, while the railway is marginalized as the mode of transport for the masses. The railway station is situated well outside the ideal city and can only be reached by car. The idea was to create a city that was both dignified and monumental. Meanwhile, workers' villages like Nucleo Bandeirante, suburbs, and satellite towns appeared which had "never been part of any plan."[9]

Tractorization!

The crisis that hit the ideal city was not the outcome of any specific system; it struck in the West as much as in functioning socialist states that had always subordinated town planning to the production processes and the ideology of a classless society. The first Soviet five-year plan was dominated by heavy industry. The revolutionaries, imposing their thinking from above, became intoxicated by the idea of transforming the outdated agrarian regions into a "land of metal," as Stalin put it, into a land dominated by the automobile, a "land of tractorization."[10] The industrial city came into being, and thousands of experts fled the economic crisis engulfing the Western world and sought refuge in the apparently booming Soviet Union. Amongst them was Ernst May, who was later to be appointed director of urban planning for the Zekombank. "No one can tell whether this greatest political experiment of all time will be a success,"[11] wrote May in 1930. And while Fordism became the model for socialist industrial politics, the

American Albert Kahn, who had previously played a leading role in the formation of the automobile industry in Detroit, drew up plans for around five hundred new factories between 1930 and 1932, which were to become the main projects of the first five-year plan. On August 9, 1931, the *New York Times Magazine* reported that Avtostroj, the first Communist model city, had shot out of the ground at a speed that did Russia proud. A unique constellation: American engineers inter-preting socialist urban planning. The rows of housing near the car factory culminated in a central square that connected society and culture to the might of the state, and contained the House of the Soviets, a museum, a hospital, a department store, and a fire station. A boulevard ran from here to the airport. In 1931, Ernst May was appointed director of planning for the model city and doubled its size. If there ever was such a thing as real, physically present ideal cities under the Communist regime, then these would have to be industrial complexes, most notably Magnitorgorsk. This prototype of a socialist city was built around the most modern steelworks of its day, at the heart of a metal mining area in the Urals. Where nomads' tents had once stood, the state built a settlement for 50,000 people, though without kitchens in the living quarters, as canteens were intended to provide meals for the entire population. In early March 1930, a first meeting of the jury rejected the outcome of the competition for a new city, because it did not satisfactorily make provision for the desired level of socialization; the jury did, however, award two second prizes, a third, and two fourth prizes. All the submissions provided variants on the so-called compact city with residential complexes, short traffic arteries, and copious green areas between the city and the factory. But things took a different turn. Ernst May stepped in; the city grew to a population of 80,000 and continued to grow until it had 200,000 inhabitants. A later commission harshly criticized May's plans, which were little different from capitalist urban planning with high-density accommodation to the detriment of the population's health. In the spring of 1931, May left the Zekombank, having

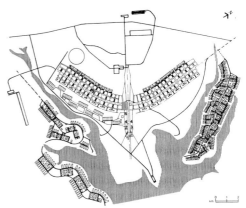

Lucio Costa, Plan for Brasilia, 1957

forfeited his "hitherto leading position in the field of socialist urban planning."[12] And Magnitorgorsk, the much-hyped ideal, never lived up to the high expectations invested in it. In the late 1930s, nameless housing schemes and camp-like hous-ing sprang up close to the steelworks. Everything was concentrated in Moscow, which under Stalin was beautified with gingerbread architecture. Such socialism as there was had to drop its high-flying plans; prefabricated blocks came to dominate housing, and industrial complexes rusted away after the Iron Curtain had been swept aside.

Moving Pictures

For some years now our horizons have been widen-ing. The West has been looking to the East, where China is poised to make huge strides forwards. In the midst of the anarchic upheavals obliterating the boundaries between town and country, we find Luchao, a circular city with a lake at its center. It sounds like a postmodern paradox, with a non-existent center and a stage-managed void. A perfectly circular lake shimmers precisely where one would expect to find the city at its densest. Urban life has shifted into a sequence of rings, each with a view of the artificial lake. Bridges and ferries connect six landmarks. The Atoll of

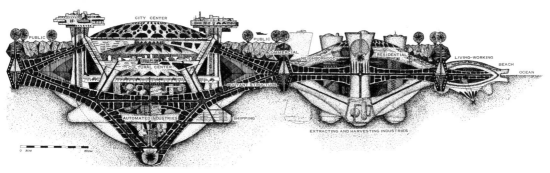

Novanoah, one of Paolo Soleri's utopian cities, 1964

Knowledge, the House of the Currents, and the Island of Work veer from the metaphorical to the reality of their actual construction: a new version of Plato's radial city of Atlantis, enriched by ideas drawn from Ebenezer Howard's early-twentieth-century garden city. Urban life is no longer dependent on a city center; it is played out in equal-value districts situated around the ring-shaped thoroughfares. Swathes of green separate residential districts; town and country interlock but do not invade each other. The divisions are distinct, the boundaries are clear. In the center, there is no "best room" as there is in Siena— surrounded by perforated facades and grand buildings—but a stage made of sand and water, perfectly circular and multi-functional. The central business district encircles the lake.

China thinks in pictures, so in their presentation the Hamburg architects von Gerkan, Marg und Partner (GMP) talked of "Luchao—born from a droplet" and showed the dance of a single drop of water. Concentric circles spread out from its point of contact with the water. This formed the basis of the notion of a bionic city that takes its signature from natural processes. The architects' declared aim was "to make a city fit for human beings, in full knowledge of how ideals were subverted in Brasilia and Chandigarh." Luchao is to point the way from the city built to accommodate the automobile to the city built for human beings. This constitutes a departure from modernist thinking: the car takes second place, as though town planners could pre-empt the European experience with private vehicles that China still has to go through. In the meantime, East and West lock

horns on the test bed of the third modernity. And the results are not just solid buildings but, above all, moving pictures that attest to China's new beginnings. Speed is of the essence on Chinese construction sites. The plans have become waste paper even before the plotters have spat them out. Barely had GMP presented the concept of Luchao at a major exhibition when the plans had been revised. The population had tripled by decree. Now 800,000—not 300,000—were to populate the new harbor city. The circular design had grown another ring and two offshoots on the other side of Downtown, as the original city is now known. In addition, there is now also a 2.5-mile-long (4 km) green belt, a Leisure City with a harbor atmosphere, and more space for small businesses in the west.

Chinese City Continuum

Ideal cities were not invented in the Occident. China already knew all about them even before the Romans carried its civilization across the Alps and, with their fortresses, sowed the seeds of later medieval towns. To quote the Frankfurt town planner Albert Speer, "The main difference is that the Chinese city is a continuum. All the upheavals in Chinese history have never affected the basic principle: the north-south axis, with a palace at its midway point and a regular urban layout around it." There is a key to the Chinese notion of the city in the shape of one particular Chinese character. "Zhong" means both "center" and "town." It consists of a square divided across the center by a

von Gerkan, Marg und Partner, Luchao Harbor City, Shanghai, China, competition 2002–03

single line. This was exactly the structure under-pinning the design of Chinese towns, laid out according to a clear grid. The town itself is divided into four quarters, each side of which is a Chinese mile long (around 1,300 feet (400 m)). Each quarter has trading streets, squares, and a temple complex. Luchao has not only replaced the square with the Platonic circle, it has also attempted to give the ideal city an ecological anchor. In the center, there is the park; in the center of each block, there are traffic-free zones, places for people to congregate and interact. Ideal proportions, grids, and rules are applied, contain-ing an otherwise uncontrollable organic growth. Life needs more than good planning. Already the geometric clarity of the residential districts is threatening to disappear; the good locations in the green belts are too tempting. It's already in the cards that soon they will be occupied by high-density high-rises. Ideal cities are not compatible with a dynamically developing world.

1 As quoted in *DU 742 Utopisches Bauen*, December 2003, p.50.
2 Virgilio Vercelloni, *Atlante storico dell'idea europea della città ideale* (Milan, 1994), plate 140.
3 Charles Delfante, *Grand histoire de la ville: de la Mésopotamie aux Etats-Unis* (Paris, 1997).
4 As quoted in Ruth Eaton, *Ideal cities: Utopianism and the (Un)Built Environment* (London, 2002).
5 To quote a comment in 1963 by his former colleague Walter Gropius at the Bauhaus. As quoted in Eaton, *Ideal Cities*.
6 See note 3 above.
7 Kenneth Frampton, *Modern Architecture: A Critical History* (London, 1980), p.155.
8 Ibid.
9 See note 3 above.
10 Joseph Stalin, "Das Jahr des großen Umschwungs," in idem, *Fragen des Leninismus* (Moscow, 1938), p.411. As quoted in Harald Bodenschatz and Christiane Post, *Städtebau im Schatten Stalins: Die internationale Suche nach der sozialistischen Stadt in der Sowjetunion 1929–1935* (Berlin, 2003), p.27.
11 Ernst May, "Warum ich Frankfurt verlasse" (Why I'm Leaving Frankfurt), in *Frankfurter Zeitung*, August 1, 1930. As quoted in ibid., p.33.
12 Bodenschatz, *Städtebau im Schatten Stalins*, p.63.

THEMING A WORLD
Theory and Practice of Architainment

Heirs to the ideal city are themed environments that focus on single aspects of traditional urban communities—security (gated communities), pleasure (amusement parks), or commerce (malls)—and inflate these into self-contained dream worlds that exist without any urban context. They are their own centers. The only thing that matters is access to the infrastructure of highways and airfields; cars, and increasingly airplanes, connect autonomous worlds which are springing up across the globe, all conforming to universal standards. With city centers in a state of decay and suburbs going downhill, these dream worlds were to become the cultural paradigm of the late-twentieth century. The urban *civitas*, where bourgeois society functions on the basis of the interchange of diverse interests, becomes the perfectly planned and marketed, temporary private meeting place.

Theming has been astonishingly successful; nowadays whole departments of marketing specialists, sociologists, and town planners devote their entire energies to adapting displays, rooms, buildings, and recently even whole towns to highlight the single aspect that is to optimize their competitiveness in the battle for that scarce resource, attention. However diverse the ideas, slogans, and fashions, the strategies are always much the same. Any place can be presented— in an especially memorable and unmistakable manner—as an experience, and at the same time it can convey a sense of protection and security, which culminates in an ethos of repetition: department store chains, brand names, and labels.

While branding gives major companies a self-contained visual and semantic frame of reference theming translates this practice into rooms, buildings, streets, and whole landscapes. These become closed worlds where the basic formative elements—colors, surfaces, textures, or shapes— are subsumed, like pieces in a mosaic, into a higher category: spatial effect, overall design, and user-friendliness. Nothing is left to chance since the design is all about generating good vibrations in the clients, who in their precious leisure time visit so-called urban entertainment centers.

This applies not only where one would expect it—in leisure complexes and theme parks—but also in situations or surroundings which have become part of daily life—in shopping malls, water parks, and so-called urban entertainment centers. One architect in particular has turned his attention to the visual and spatial design of locations that appear to be semi-public but are in fact wholly private: Jon Jerde, based in Venice, California, creates virtuosic shopping worlds for clients across the globe.

Urban Dreamland Design

It all started with the Horton Plaza in San Diego in 1977. Jon Jerde Associates created an urban landscape which Dietmar Steiner, Director of the Center for Architecture in Vienna, has described with open admiration as an "urban dreamland with clean roadways, surprising bridges, bizarre facades and vulgar shapes."[1] Clean, surprising,

The Jerde Partnership, Horton Plaza, San Diego, California, 1985

bizarre, vulgar—it takes a moment's thought to recognize that this is the same ambiguity Robert Venturi was looking for in 1966 in *Complexity and Contradiction in Architecture*.[2] Jerde developed this into his own strategy of "carefully calculated confusion,"[3] which is designed to meet the need of commerce, stimulate the senses, and provide just a handful of contradictions to serve as intentional stumbling blocks in the normally smooth-running, safe world of shopping. The qualities defined by Venturi—perceptual possibilities—are now part of the currency of skilful marketing which has descended on whole town centers and even replaces them, as is occurring in the United States. As well-ordered, clean, safe zones, malls and theme parks do in fact embody the very qualities that many of us wish to see in public spaces.

Successful themed environments aim to create a self-contained, secure, and pleasant (clean) situation. And yet, very few have mastered the real art of theming, where intentional non sequiturs, in the end, have an optically stimulating effect. It is much simpler to isolate individual aspects and optimize them, as chain stores do. They both instigate and benefit from the development of readymade consumer goods into just such consumer environments. Nothing differentiates a good burger chain so much as its ability to replicate its products. Once developed and promoted, the product must look exactly the same and be prepared in exactly the same way in every situation and in every country; but, above all, it has to taste the same. Surprise beyond the "carefully calculated confusion" is the enemy of easygoing consumption. This principle applies in most themed spaces, which are designed first and foremost as entertainment. Franchise chains like Burger King, Hard Rock Cafe, Planet Hollywood, and Starbucks should be immediately recognizable by their look, even if this is regularly revised. Color-coding and design manuals mean that the new is instantly old.

Of course, much seems artificial in themed environments. The walls have a hollow ring and the materials seem deceptively real; but these scenarios for distraction are not intended to create a sense of authenticity, but rather their highest aim is to provide the right "stage," an atmospheric setting, or the perfect ambience. The focus is on softer factors, on intangible feelings which architecture has always had trouble dealing with as soon as its ambition has nothing to do with monumentality, sanctity, or sheer power. Potemkin villages or simulated environments are better settings for fun and games, for shopping as a leisure activity. As Rem Koolhaas once said, "Luna Park is the first manifestation of a curse that is to haunt the architectural profession for the rest of its life, the formula: technology + cardboard (or any other flimsy material) = reality."[4] Anyone who gets all worked up about Disney World may have forgotten that this is where people perfected the formula for making money off an atmosphere, leading to numerous copies and half-baked concepts in the surrounding area. Drive to Orlando these days and you will see small-scale attractions growing up along International Drive: miniature golf with volcanoes and floodlighting, dinner with pirates, and virtual reality sports at WonderWorks. The boundaries of the park have long since been breached by entertainment which invades every area of life and which, with its light shows and other attractions, celebrates even the most trivial aspect of daily life as an experience.

City vs. Site

The customer now reigns supreme. And when customers find they lack adventures of their own, they resort to the prepackaged adventures available from a highly developed leisure industry. If we are to believe the sociologist Gerhard Schulze, in recent decades society has developed "a thirst for adventure as the new collective baseline motivation."[5] People wish to fill their lives with positive experiences, sculpting their existences just as they would a physically fit body. Even the most banal activity must be presented as enjoyable; old acts and rituals are revalued and endowed with new attributes. The old dream of a better life takes on a new consumerist gloss: every shopping trip an experience, every dinner a candlelit

Entrance to Legoland, Günzburg, Germany

adventure. Theming means selling. Nowadays we find ourselves in brand-name worlds that designers have created around a particular core—the product—in order to position them as emotional experiences or adventures.

Legoland and Nike Town do not limit themselves to Lego bricks, sneakers, or sportswear, but turn their products into an experience, by surrounding them with a context and a history, enriched, for example, by auratic items actually worn by famous athletes. But aura and authenticity are only on loan and have to be constantly adjusted to suit the time. Corporate image centers, on the other hand, like the Sony Center at Potsdamer Platz in Berlin, bring together under one roof—in this case a tented roof above a 43,000-square-foot (4,000 m^2) plaza—a multiplex cinema, an Imax theater, specialty restaurants, and the corporation's European headquarters. The most recent offshoots of the entertainment universe combine consumption and entertainment with image promotion, meaning a location does not necessarily have to be profitable by itself—all that matters is its promotional value.

Private vs. Public Space

Urban entertainment centers, malls, and hermetically sealed parks outside the city have a dramatic effect on public spaces. They become mere temporary collecting grounds. Privately owned environments on the other hand adopt the guise of public spaces. This in turn has consequences on what the public can do there—and what they cannot. Critics of the new leisure oases fear the creeping erosion of public life and democratic rights, seeing this as an extension of gated communities.

"Regular shopping malls in America are awful," says Jon Jerde, "but that's where public life takes place, where you find public spaces".[6] The parallel example of Brazil has proved the guru of the event world right. For the middle classes, shopping malls are about much more than just shopping, as Wolfgang Kunath reports:

"The whole family meets there for Sunday lunch, you meet your friends there for a beer and a pizza, and young people date there. You can just wander around, letting time pass, going to the cinema, the theater, a gallery, a bookshop, the hairdressers, the dentist, or make a visit to the plastic surgeon; you can have your car washed and waxed, tone your stomach muscles, or dance away the hours in a disco."[7] These autonomous worlds grow and form bubbles next to other bubbles of our highly differentiated society, scarcely ever touching each other and certainly never mingling. For "shopping is part of the private art-public which is proliferating in Brazil in step with decay and criminality: high-security zones, with parking lots where you can jog in safety in the mornings—although not without paying—before the flood of customers arrives."[8]

It's easy to condemn these developments, as many critics do—describing theme parks as reflections of American-style capitalism and imperialism or as places of extreme social control which quash any hope the visitor might have had of participation, spontaneity, or creative appropriation.[9] At the same time, there is a huge demand for safe, clean, and comfortable shopping facilities, factory outlet centers on green meadows, and changing, increasingly extravagant modes of presentation. In view of the overwhelming superficiality of any experience one might have there, it is easy to dismiss this aesthetic as false or escapist, and yet Umberto Eco acknowledges Disneyland as an "Absolute Fake."[10] No longer out to confuse what people see with reality, the perfect fake is presented as something admirable in its own right.

Theming as Displaced Perception

Theming instigates a displaced perception of the world and sense of reality that is only surpassed by the 3-D animations currently making the leap from simulation to the generation of whole worlds and modes of perception. And even if, as Jean Baudrillard has suggested, this development is towards ever-greater artificiality, it is nevertheless also a process of civilization which is increasingly replacing the world with its own images. But is that really as new and as fatal as the critics say; critics who set store by a reality which, at least since the advent of modernism, has had such fundamental doubt cast upon it that by now it is little more than ideology and nostalgic remembrance? All those years ago, Hieronymus Bosch's *Apocalypse* envisioned hell on earth, for it seems that nothing worries human beings more than the fears, fantasies, and machines that they themselves have created.

Disneyland, to name but one classic development, exploits the symbols of reality in a highly creative manner. These are turned into over-optimal signs—artistically and almost subversively—which, wherever they appear, are immediately recognized, and elicit a response—mostly in the form of lines outside the entrance. That is the other displacement that theming induces: the world becomes a sign to be decoded, rather than an adventure playground to be discovered and explored.

Now it would be wrong to inquire as to the function of theming without taking into account the monetary and performative services—affirming the status quo—that they fulfill for major concerns, who thereby extend their own market. But it seems that an even more important factor is its significance for society, which is starting to break free of some of its traditions and living in more of a cultural mix, at least superficially. And this is perfectly served by theming. The scenarios themselves are hardly groundbreaking; on the contrary, they are calculated investments, often deploying the elements of successful Hollywood blockbusters, trusting in simple recipes rather than questioning modes of reception. In his study, *The Theming of America*, Mark Gottdiener comes to the sobering conclusion that innovation takes second place to existing formulas, to the "recycling of the arcade, the state fair, the world exposition, and the ambiance of the cosmopolitan, pedestrian city ... Realization that the indulgence in fantasy environments consists of a limited repertoire that in many ways apes Hollywood cinema is, perhaps, the biggest disappointment."[11]

Theming is a growth market and the industry has its own Oscar, the Thea Award, which is given annually to the best performer by the Themed Entertainment Association—thus confirming its affinity to Hollywood—to dream worlds made from plywood and *papier-maché*—and more recently with the help of computer software. The end product is ideal, placeless, self-referential, omnipresent, and attractive. It is now everyday reality for many people to meet in themed locations—in these semi-public spaces—because there are no other properly functioning places of assembly. Themed environments have long since become part of our own environment, easily comprehended worlds in an age of upheaval and uncertainty. Whether they will outdo the city and render it superfluous, or whether they themselves will be sucked into the increased urbanism of our time, is yet to be seen.

1 Dietmar Steiner, "Ein völlig normaler Mensch: Jon Jerde, Prophet des neuen öffentlichen Raumes," in *DU 742 Utopisches Bauen*, December 2003: 28–31, p.29.
2 Robert Venturi, *Complexity and Contradiction in Architecture* (New York, 1966), p.20.
3 See note 1 above.
4 Rem Koolhaas, *Delirious New York: A Retroactive Manifesto for Manhattan* (New York, 1994), p.42.
5 Gerhard Schulze, *Die Erlebnis-Gesellschaft: Kultursoziologie der Gegenwart* (Frankfurt/Main, 2000), p.192.
6 Steiner, "Jon Jerde," p.30.
7 Wolfgang Kunath, "Joggen auf bewachtem Parkplatz," *Frankfurter Rundschau* August 7, 2004
8 Ibid.
9 Regina Bormann, "'Spaß ohne Grenzen'. Kulturtheoretische Reflexionen über einen europäischen Themenpark," in *Sociologia Internationalis*, no. 36, 1998: 33–60, p.39.
10 Umberto Eco, *Travels in Hyperreality*, trans. William Weaver (San Diego CA, 1990), p.40.
11 Mark Gottdiener, *The Theming of America: Dreams, Visions, and Commercial Spaces* (Boulder, Colorado and Oxford, UK, 1997), pp.151f.

Murphy / Jahn Architects,
Sony Center, Berlin,
Germany, 2000

CELEBRATION
AND
ARCOSANTI
Urban Laboratories

Of course, Disney! Who else would find the strength in a world of contradictions, growing social conflict, and fading utopias to guarantee something approaching community and to answer the big question: how do we want to live? The fabulous rise and abrupt decline of the ideal city in the twentieth century is directly connected with the ideologies it embodies. Once the Cold War was over, the grass was no longer greener on the other side of the curtain; utopias lost their appeal and society, which had relished experiment in the 1960s, now preferred to insulate itself and return to familiar forms and formulas. Of all people, in the mid-1960s it was Disney who came up with EPCOT, the Experimental Prototype Community of Tomorrow, which consists of an airport, a leisure park, and a residential area, taking up and advancing the modernist city with its separated functions. Traffic was to have run underground, separated according to speed and type of vehicle. So it seems today that Celebration is the legitimate heir to EPCOT: "Here the pedestrian will be king, free to walk and browse without fear of motorized vehicles. Only electric powered vehicles will travel above the streets of EPCOT's central city."[1] Perhaps Celebration is simply an EPCOT cut down to normal size, without the dreams, yet still seeking an alternative to the urban sprawl, the bleak reality of anonymous suburbs, and run-down downtowns. Founded by Disney in 1994, Celebration has not only visually signed on to the good old days, it also seeks to replicate the closed society of a village that has no desire whatsoever to grow into a town. The ideal of helpful neighbors, an authentic Main Street—free of national chains—and beautiful housing was simply an extension of the atmosphere of good fun for the whole family that had long been tested at Disney World. But this development according to the principles of "New Urbanism" was not without its detractors. The United States itself produces the sharpest critics of its own American Way of Life: Paolo Soleri for one, with his experimental town of Arcosanti (founded in 1970), wants to create an alternative to the decentralized city constructed on a completely inhuman scale. Yet Soleri's dream seems more like a freeze-dried utopia from the 1960s: monumental and lifeless.

previous double pages: Panorama of Arcosanti

Celebration, Florida: white houses, clean streets, and a cloudless sky.

On Main Street, the shopping arcades are filled with music from recessed loudspeakers.

Aldo Rossi's office
park on the outskirts
of Celebration.

Celebration—
The Town That Wants To Be a Village

Main Street, Celebration. Dixieland music spills out of street-level speakers and swirls
around passers-by. On Saturday morning there's not much going on under the arcades
leading to the lake, past Gooding's General Store and Dolls, the doll shop. A breeze wafts
through the plane trees, waves lap up against the quay, and deckchairs invite one to
linger a while. Paradise is celebrating its birthday. Ten years of Celebration. Ten years
of life in a perfect world on the edge of Disney World in Orlando, Florida.

In 1994, the Walt Disney Company founded this synthetic small town. "New Urbanism" was the magic formula the entertainment giant used to create this miniature world.
Robert Stern, a professor at Yale University, drew up the master plan as an answer to faceless suburbs: a vision of densely packed, quaint little houses with front porches and gardens,
surrounded by water and parks. A picture-book retro-idyll with precise rules for the way the
inhabitants are to live together, with no room for chain stores and certainly no Disney souvenirs. The center is a model of postmodernism. Everyone who is anyone has built something
here: Aldo Rossi, Michael Graves, Robert Stern, Charles W. Moore, Robert Venturi, Philip
Johnson, and Cesar Antonio Pelli. The town is supposed to look perfectly normal, which is
what makes its restrained colors and "classical" doorways appear so contrived. What Main
Street was to good old Uncle Walt in 1955—a fading memory of an ideal of community life,

Speculating on the future: Celebration is growing and growing and growing.

friendly neighbors, and helpful shop owners—is what Celebration strives to be for the average American in the 1990s: clean, safe, and above all far removed from the jostling crowds of the big city with its sprawling neighborhoods and unattractive malls.

Electric vehicles purr down the streets; everything is so well ordered here that the Sheriff becomes bored doing his rounds. Nothing much happens in paradise, where a flea market is proudly proclaimed and the *Celebration News* lists by name all those volunteering at the library. People know each other, we are to assume, exactly as had been promised in the Disney brochures: "Have you ever wanted to be part of something bigger than yourself?" This appeals to the middle classes. The houses are inexpensive, the front gardens luscious, the lawns—perfectly trimmed greens—have the vigor of grass ready for the Super Bowl. Rick is content. "Nice and tidy," remarks the bulky Texan and steps towards the paving stones that lie like a red carpet between the path and the road. Rick is accompanying his fiancée on a visit to his future parents-in-law. Before that, they go to see the model of this big little town. In the show house on Beak Street there is an artificial world within an artificial world: like liver-shaped islands, new clones of Celebration extend into the surrounding, undeveloped forest. Newly-opened districts of the town with winding streets are fringed by artificial lakes. So would he like to live here? Rick straightens his sunglasses. "Not really," he says, "not enough space between the houses," and adds, almost apologetically, "We're from Texas, we're not stuck right next to our neighbors there."

An American Utopia

American utopias need sun if they are to prosper. They need dreamy evenings, a SUV in front of the house, and a pool behind it. Celebration doesn't have that. No splashing of private fountains, and the plots are more like green towels than racing tracks for motorized mowers. Yet, despite this, Celebration sells its houses like hot cakes, because it has one very important thing to offer: a comfortable, manageable life of the kind our great-grandparents might have led. With 2,736 inhabitants at the start of the new millennium, this artificial town has since eaten up large swathes of the subtropical forest. As though

Progress travels by electromobile: this compact town encourages neighborliness.

they were wielding giant hedge shears, the town developers have cut new districts from the untamed brush. The pioneers of this intact world leave nothing to chance. Barely has an artificial clearing been created then they ram street signs into the sand like gold-diggers' claims; soon flower beds will appear there, town houses, and paved sidewalks, while the parks department plants the first bushes and shrubs.

The town is booming. There were 8,000 people in 2004, and the plan is that by 2010 there will be no less than 20,000; apparently, Disney is planning to spend 4 billion dollars in total.[2] In a few years Celebration could well have reached the limits of its idyllic village atmosphere. More inhabitants not only mean greater distances but also, above all, will increase the complexity of a system that relies on simple solutions and clear rules. But Celebration is never supposed to become a real town, with good and not-so-good areas. It has no locked entrances barring the way to gated communities, no walls, no security guards in evidence. This function is served by Celebration Boulevard, which runs along the northern edge of the town like a green dyke. Somewhere beyond the other world begins, with its malls and highways. There are no cars on the boulevard, just two or three Mexican workers trimming the median strip. California must once have been like this, some-time back in the 1940s, when the skies were still boundless. Optimism in Celebration means that at intervals of 110 yards (100 m), side streets lead off the boulevard into the under-growth. At some point in the future, white family homes will stand here with porches where the new citizens will sit when the cool evening breeze kicks up. The construction process seems to take no time at all. Where subtropical forest stood not so long ago, we now see Artisan Park, the latest offshoot of Celebration.

Pick Your Color

The signs with the street names are already in place: Craftsman Avenue, Tapestry Drive, Mosaic Drive. First lilac, then dove-gray, and lastly royal red—the income brackets of the new residents are colorfully depicted on the foldout map of Celebration. Each color denotes a price category: $100,000 for a residence in Terrace Home, $200,000 for the Garden Home with a steep gable and a porch, upwards of $800,000 for a dream in white in the shape of a Southern States villa, available in Colonial, Victorian, Classical, Coastal, French, or Mediterranean style, all with white columns and a mighty portico.

Celebration is not the nadir of the history of the town, just a place where time has been made to stand still, a place that

With its wild mix of styles, Celebration is at odds with an otherwise supremely egalitarian society.

is trying to adopt the looks of yesteryear in order to counter the development of car-friendly aggregate conurbations. In its design, it reflects the American middle classes' attempts to flee faceless suburbs and decaying city centers. In return, they gladly accept boredom and control, the corollaries of order and security. And everything fits here. Even the stop signs in the newly built Celebration Village are beige, not red—beige like the facades of the apartments owned by the residents. What was it Jim Carrey was told in the movie *The Truman Show*, that everything was true, that nothing he was seeing in the series was fake, that there was just a certain degree of control? In fact, the idea of control fits well in dream worlds where each neighborhood is minutely regulated and where every blade of grass looks freshly painted and formed. At Roseville Corner, two gigantic trees bend towards each other across the street, forming a natural gateway. Next to them, stumps rise up out of the ground and a snake slithers across the asphalt. And, like in a fairytale, the dream of a better world has a catch that cuts deeply into one's flesh: instead of an elected mayor, the Town Hall is occupied by a Town Manager. But it doesn't bother the town's inhabitants; on the contrary, they will proudly tell you about the two schools in Celebration, their 18-hole golf course, their fire department, and their very respectable Celebration Hotel. In mid-January 2004, Disney sold the town center to Lexin Capital. The realtors immediately announced that basically nothing would be changed. Celebration was to stay as it is: awesomely beautiful.

Arcosanti—the Frugal Utopia

To understand Arcosanti you have to drive through Phoenix, seventy miles away.
Expressways cut through the desert; parking lots, billboards, houses, and strip malls
form a shapeless urban landscape. No trace of a center. Naturally, there is the obliga-
tory downtown with its high-rise buildings; there is even a landmark, or rather two:
the Camelbacks. But these are no more than bare hills in a sea of parking lots, shops,
and streets. In just twenty years, Phoenix has doubled in size. The motorized American
dream is here for all to see, including manicured lawns and backyard pools. It is as
though Frank Lloyd Wright's 1932 vision had materialized: Broadacre City, the decentralized city of the West. Phoenix has just 2,750 people per square mile, and everything is easily accessible by car. And Phoenix is still growing.

    Suddenly there are no more buildings. One last billboard, and then the Arizona
Desert opens up. Red sand and fissured slopes interspersed with cacti and dusty
prairie grass. The land rises up to a height of 3,750 feet (1,143 m). At Cordes
Junction, halfway between Phoenix and Flagstaff, lies an example diametrically
opposed to the breath-taking lateral proliferation of cities in the American West:
Arcosanti, as compact as a Tuscan village, a place for pedestrians and visionaries
built according to plans developed by the architect and philosopher Paolo Soleri.
"Urban Laboratory" is written on a sign the height of a man down below the highway.

Arcosanti draws people in with a café, a baker's shop, guest rooms, a gift shop, and Soleri windbells.

A 2.5-mile-long (4 km) dust track takes you to the visitors' car park up above the Agua Fria River Valley. Not a soul in sight. Arcosanti looks like a movie set while the crew is on break. Pines sway in the evening breeze, and long shadows move across walls that have bunches of grass and rusting metal ends protruding from them. Crazily parked cars and piles of building materials convey quite the opposite impression to a utopia. To the left a crane creaks between steel building components and sections of concrete, to the right is the visitors' center, built in 1977, a five-story block with square oriel windows a bit like the machicolations on a medieval fortress. Soleri combined a number of architectural languages in Arcosanti.

Concrete Circles in the Sun

Here we see echoes of Paul Rudolph's Faculty of Architecture in New Haven with its cyclopic, vertically divided facades; over there, the whimsical Nakagin Capsule Tower in Tokyo with its bull's-eye windows. Inside the square cafeteria we see the influence of Soleri's favorite builder, Louis Kahn. Concrete circles with glass set into them rise up to the height of two floors. They invite us to let our gaze roam across the Mesa. Arcosanti lies like an Inca fortress above the Agua Fria, a rivulet trickling between dusty bushes. Beside the visitor center are the semi-spheres of the ceramics workshop and foundry. These richly decorated arcs reach a height of over 26 feet (8 m), like the remnants of some mysterious cult. In the summer the south-facing apses provide shade, in the winter they gather in the warming rays of the sun like opened hands. More than twice their height, the airy concrete arches of the South and North Vault shoot straight up into the sky. These two buildings form the heart of Arcosanti, a roofed piazza for all the hustle and bustle of daily life. But

Like an ancient fossil on a mesa in North Arizona: Paolo Soleri's dream city of Arcosanti.

at the moment, only eighty "Arcosantis" live and work here—eighty out of a hoped-for five thousand inhabitants. The realized buildings in the model look like toys.

Soleri's visions were always somehow immoderate, as though the town planner wanted to translate the expanses of the American West directly into drawings. In the model, the vaults of Market Square disappear under cyclopean residential high-rises; Arcosanti spreads over 25 acres (10 hectares). That is the wonderful contradiction of this town that has become an eternal construction site. Arcosanti owes its greatness above all to the idea behind its sculptural buildings. On paper the Italian-American shows whole districts of high-rise homes: Mesa City, a sea of tulip houses with hundred of thousands living and working there; or Novanoah, a floating town just off the coast. Service tracts and elevators connect helipads and viewing balustrades; automated factories are banished into the deepest underground levels of the metropolis. In reality, the crane creaks. Soleri's drawings give an impression of the topsy-turvy 1960s: sketches breathed onto the paper with a rapidograph, where one's gaze loses its way as in a mandala. Crosshatchings and interlocking details lead us into ever-deeper layers of thought. Soleri's drawings made him famous. He himself calls these urban centers, condensed into the smallest of spaces, "arcologies": ecological architecture as the antidote to the sprawling cities of the United States. Soleri, a trained architect with a doctorate from Turin University, was twenty-eight when, in 1947, he went to join Frank Lloyd Wright, the greatest architect-builder of his time. In Taliesin West, he got to know the desert and a community that believed in a better world, while on the horizon Phoenix was swelling to become a city of millions. A year later Soleri fell out with Wright, and founded his own utopia laboratory Cosanti, in Paradise Valley near Phoenix.

Soleri touched a nerve with the early hippies. His stance was anti-consumerist: he lauded the simple life in densely built, un-American looking towns. Success greeted his efforts. *Visionary Architecture* was the name of his major MoMA exhibition in October 1960. In a stroke, the wiry, forty-one-year-old architect was rubbing shoulders with

Piranesi, Le Corbusier, Buckminster Fuller, and Louis Kahn. Soleri had the same ability as Kahn to make grand gestures, and shared his preference for arches and openings. Both were striving to create a *Gesamtkunstwerk*. As Soleri once said of Kahn: "He was the only one who really interested me." But he was never able to entirely shake off the influence of the great modernists. Look closely at the stacked discs of the high-rises of Novanoah and you will find echoes of Frank Lloyd Wright's Guggenheim Museum. *Time Magazine* called Soleri "Dream Builder," and in 1970, in just that capacity, he started work on his greatest dream: Arcosanti.

The central meeting place in Arcosanti for summer festivals and intimate gatherings alike.

A City to Save the World

"The project has been a series of highs and lows," to quote Mary Hoadley, site-coordinator for Arcosanti. "In the 1980s, when there were just three dozen students here each year, progress was incredibly slow." Hoadley, with a degree in anthropology, first encountered Soleri in 1970. "We wanted to save the world," says Hoadley, "we thought we could build Arcosanti in five years." Hundreds of volunteers slaved away to make that better world, and Arcosanti became a tent city of optimists. The square visitor center was finished, as were the barrel vaults of the market place and the amphitheatre. In the mid-1970s the builders found their energy running out, the number of student volunteers decreased, and the crane, a sign pointing to the future, became a symbol of stagnation.

The last tour of the day has just begun. Bernadette O'Neill is guiding seven tourists through the settlement. Bernadette is wearing a fleece jacket and has her hair in a pageboy cut. She has lived here for the last eighteen years. In Arcosanti the aesthetics of the 1960s still live on, bull's-eye windows and round doors gaze out of apartment blocks, the complex itself forms a semicircle around the amphitheatre; the balconies become theatrical boxes, the verandas bring people together. The tourists march across concrete slabs towards the market-place, two concrete barrel vaults big enough to contain three detached houses. Red and yellow stripes adorn their walls like a huge tattoo. "This is where we party," says Bernadette, "there's plenty of room here," opening her arms in an uncertain gesture of welcome. Closer to the slope is the ceramic apse, a semi-spherical form, over 16 feet (5 m) high, open to the south, with decorative panels set into the roof arches. Boxes full of clay stamps and bell shapes stand around in disarray. Bernadette makes these bizarrely shaped ceramic bells herself. Single pieces can cost up to three hundred dollars; less complicated Soleri windbells can be bought for under a third of that. These much sought-after souvenirs help to finance a dedicated community that lives from a small amount of agriculture and a great deal of enthusiasm. Thanks to the bells, the Cosanti Foundation and Cosanti Originals have a yearly budget of around $900,000.

Arcosanti has long since become a cult destination, like Frank Lloyd Wright's summer school at Taliesin near Phoenix,

an anti-world to the American urban sprawl. The rest goes to the good cause. Even Soleri doesn't get more than eight dollars when he designs new bells or designs new extensions to buildings. Arcosanti is his life's work, his legacy. Over 6,000 students, dropouts, and architecture freaks have helped to build this dream. To date, 9.5 million dollars worth of materials and labor have been poured into the domes and towers of the desert city. Each week Soleri spends two days inspecting his dream town. He talks in a quiet, monotonous voice, as though he were repeating himself for the thousandth time, while he fixes you with his alert gaze. As though he were addressing a university audience, the philosopher in sandals and linen pants delivers a lecture decrying urban sprawl, the way that cities consume land, senseless transportation routes, and monotonous suburbs. For almost fifty years, he has fought these in his writings and in his drawings, creating huge castles in the sky. Perhaps that is why it seems that Arcosanti has been built for Titans. And then he stops and adds that beauty is nothing other than simplicity. Soleri has spent many a long year refining this philosophy. By now Arcosanti has become a virtual community, with members all over the world, a state of mind that goes far beyond the construction site in Arizona. And this is precisely the source of its strength, not its hastily built barrel vaults and domes, which brood in the Arizona sun like gigantic stage sets.

1   http://www.waltopia.com/florida_film.html
2   "Celebration is costing Disney $4 billion to build in Florida. It will have 20,000 inhabitants, with a chic downtown built by some of the world's leading architects and neighbourhoods that try to turn back the clock to a golden age of white picket fences and neatly trimmed lawns." Broadcast by the BBC on June 4, 1996.

The entrances to the living cells at Arcosanti call to mind Hobbit-holes.

CONEY ISLAND AND THE OKTOBERFEST
Amusement Archetypes

previous double pages:
The Oktoberfest in Munich
at night

Terminus. The subway has carried its passengers out of Manhattan, rattling its way through Brooklyn with the promise of wide horizons by the sea. But the sky remains overcast, hanging leaden over Coney Island. Down below the elevated subway station, M&H Discounts has everything you need for the beach, and what you don't buy there you can get at Mermaid Horizon, a shop selling more beach items that sits opposite the boarded-up Terminal Hotel on Stillwell Avenue. The time has long gone when people would indulge in small pleasures by the sea, and nothing is sadder than a cold, wet day at the beach. The booths are barricaded shut, the sand is damp, and the beach promenade is slippery; along Reigelmann Boardwalk, where police cars are on patrol, warning signs hang crookedly on the wall: "No dressing or undressing, No combing hair over sinks. No loitering, No bottles." The joyless instructions are strangely at odds with the Coney Island of the past: a place where generations of New Yorkers went to have fun, the ones who could not afford beach houses on Long Island and who found nature on the shores of the Atlantic as well as a world of sensations and illusions, an ever-intensifying mix of exotic places and attractions.

In his famous text, *Delirious New York: A Retroactive Manifesto for Manhattan*, Rem Koolhaas called Coney Island "a fetal Manhattan." His sociological study of the city draws a parallel between the rise of the metropolis with that of the pleasure grounds; seeing the latter as the city's experimental pacesetter, not just as a vent for urban society but also as a test bed for future urbanization. In this same text, Koolhaas penned one of the finest and most influential hymns to this seaside resort: "Coney Island is the incubator for Manhattan's incipient themes and infant mythology. The strategies and mechanism that later shape Manhattan are tested in the laboratory of Coney Island before they finally leap forward to the larger island."[1] Two closely related images convey the power of the situation: that of the fetus, which holds the future within it, and that of the laboratory, which tests out, according to a specific plan and under utterly clear conditions, things that are to be realized later on a larger scale: Manhattan as an oversized amusement park with lights and alienating effects; with three-dimensional, crisscrossing currents; with towers and theatrical scenarios.

Beyond the horizon is Old Europe: the pier at Coney Island still bears traces of its onetime importance to residents of the metropolis of New York City in search of summer sunshine.

Coney Island has repeatedly reinvented itself during the course of its 175 years, alternately pointing to its qualities as a seaside resort for convalescents, a gambler's paradise, a center for horseracing, for betting, as "Sodom-by-the-Sea," and as the "Empire of the Nickel." Horrific fires in 1907, 1911, 1932, and 1944 reduced amusement parks and whole districts of the resort to dust and ashes. But for many years Coney Island managed, like a phoenix, to rebuild itself after every catastrophe, each time becoming bigger and more spectacular than before. It transformed itself from an exclusive, Victorian seaside resort, where visitors would respectably promenade along the beach, into a place for the masses seeking respite from their daily lives, becoming the main entertainment and pleasure zone for the up-and-coming metropolis that was New York City. Urbane beach hotels, like the Brighton Beach Hotel, with room for up to 5,000 guests, combined exclusivity and size, with the balance increasingly shifting towards mass-accommodation and magnitude.

Contradictions were rife in Coney Island. They seemed to be the driving force behind its existence. There was the noble, but rather distant East End, with its elegant beach hotels, promenades, flowerbeds, and manicured lawns, where equally noble society ladies and gentlemen would stroll and seek refuge from the turmoil of New York City; and then there was the honky-tonk West End or Norton Point. Between the two was the flourishing district of West Brighton, closer to Manhattan, and above all in closer contact with the needs of the masses. Following a series of successful speculative deals in real estate, the Episcopal Sunday School teacher and émigré from Ireland John Y. McKane eventually became the "architect of Coney Island,"[2] and was instrumental in turning Coney Island into a destination for pleasure-seekers. Soon the town was so filled with gambling dens, horseracing, and other dubious activities that horrified contemporaries like the Reverend A. C. Dixon took to referring to it as a "suburb of Sodom."[3]

Many particularly American stories were written here, fabulous success stories of the rise of individual entrepreneurs and show business personalities: of Cary Grant, who

appeared there as an acrobat; of Charles Feltman, whose "red hots" or hot dogs revolution-ized the American palate; or of Nathan Handwerker, who set up his Nathan's Famous on the corner of Surf and Stillwell Avenues in 1916 to revive the energies of day-trippers with a hearty piece of pork sausage and who, by the mid-1950s, had sold over 100 million hot dogs. When you get out of the subway station, it's the first place you come to. Behind it you see the amusement area that was so crucial to Coney Island for so long, or rather you will see what is left of those once flourishing pleasure grounds. Isolated giants stand there like beached whales: the wonderful Cyclone from 1927, the biggest roller coaster of its time and, with $100,000 invested into its drop of 85 feet (26 m), such a huge attraction that people were willing to stand in line for up to five hours just for one and a half minutes of excitement suspended between heaven and earth. And, nearby, the Wonder Wheel from 1920 on West 10th Street and, on the site of the onetime Steeplechase Amusement Park, the 250-foot (76 m) Parachute Jump, one of the last attractions to arrive, having moved to Coney Island in 1941 from the *Lifesaver Exhibit* at the New York World's Fair. And then of course there is the Pat Auletta Pier, which still bears its old name in brackets: Steeplechase Pier.

New Standards of Entertainment

Steeplechase Park, which opened in 1897, was to set new standards in the world of enter-tainment. The marketing genius George Tilyou made the connection between what the mar-ket offered and what the people wanted. He imported the Steeplechase Ride from England

Closed booths, abandoned rides, mothballed attractions: the fun and the excitement have gone elsewhere.

where the participants, on wooden horses, took part in an imaginary race on a track running up hill and down dale. He then combined this with amusements such as the rotating Barrel of Love, in which men and women struggled to keep their balance on a slanted floor that brought them naturally closer together, and the 54-foot-high (15 m) Dew Drop, a precursor to the Parachute Jump. In addition to these were a huge saltwater swimming pool and the biggest ballroom in New York State, to name but a few of the attractions. People were not only to be astonished and to laugh, they were to become the main players in their own fate; unusual, sophisticated mechanisms set in motion sequences of events like the stage scenery in a well-produced play. And George Tilyou knew all about the stage, having founded the Surf Theater in 1882, the first commercial theater at Coney Island. Steeplechase Park combined his theatrical experience with spectacular rides creating a unique experience which surpassed everything that had been on offer up to that point, most notably Paul Boyton's Sea Lion Park from 1895; directly behind the Elephant Hotel, it was the first to charge visitors for admission to a fenced-in park. Tilyou put up a fight. During his honeymoon in 1893, the restless manager visited the World Exhibition in Chicago where he saw the sensational 250-foot-high (76 m) wheel built by George Ferris. Tilyou immediately saw the potential of this rotating observation point; he would later add incandescent lights to his wheel and it soon became not only the leading attraction at Coney Island but also a symbol for amusement parks all over the United States. Tilyou had chutzpah: he promoted his own wheel—half the size of the Chicago wheel—as "the world's largest Ferris Wheel" and on that basis sold enough concession space to pay for the 125-foot (38 m) attraction.

With these mammoth attractions, different categories came together. Ferris wheels and roller coasters are built by engineers, while the task of the designer was concerned with the presentation of the necessary technology; and they did this by designing frameworks of columns, idiosyncratic castles, and cast-iron halls. The machine age was responsible for the mechanics; beaux-arts accounted for their appearance. But increasingly, the actual construction came to the fore as occurred with electricity: the modern delight par excellence was celebrated the world over with monuments such as the Palais de l'Electricité at the Paris World Exposition in 1900—not a building as such, but a

The seaside attractions now have a melancholic air about them.

manifesto, artificially lit around the clock. And at Coney Island, too, the air crackled with electricity.

The masses now went to amusement parks to try out modern track-systems and novel constructions; the latest in amusement became a test bed for modernity. There were more and more observation points—panoramic views from landmarks—each one seeking to outdo the next. By 1885, the Elephant Hotel was already setting new standards: a 122-foot-high (37 m) pachyderm under a canopy on Surf Avenue, surrounded by shows, saloons, and penny arcades—almost a miniature amusement park in itself. In 1876, the developer Andrew Culver bought a tower, measuring 300 feet (91.5 m), from the Philadelphia Centennial Exposition. At the time it was the tallest construction in the United States: "Bathers could ascend the tower on a steam-powered elevator and then bathe under the udders of a mechanical cow."[4] Technology showed its friendly face as the great nurturer, taking on a role that up until then had been the preserve of nature, symbolically dispensing milk from eternally full breasts. As we said, different categories came together, and the new adopted the guise of the familiar.

The bizarre mingled with prodigious technical advances, or, to put it another way: technology disguised itself as old-world mythology. The Ferris wheel tapped into medieval notions of Fortuna and the eternal cycle of becoming, growing, and withering; the roller-coaster experience on the other hand mapped out a path through the world and one's own life as a complex three-dimensional curve. It promised adventure and introduced the possibility of taking a calculated risk into the world of the workers who were increasingly tied to the rhythms of the conveyor belt, which reigned supreme in industrial production after its 1960s invention in the slaughterhouses of Cincinnati. The machine operator recuperated from his daily life in a leisure machine, and it was the burgeoning culture industry that made this possible.

The Luna Park Label

Within the space of just a few years, a whole new market for mass entertainment emerged and evolved. It stamped its leading successes as "amusement parks," a label used to denote these special pleasure grounds—separated from daily life—where one had to pay a charge for admission. Even as one stepped across the threshold, a transformation took place. While the entrance to Luna Park—"the Heart of Coney Island"—with its iron arches and two deathly obelisks still promised a rather more fabulous "world exposition," its successor, Dreamland, opened up completely new territory. Two lighthouses flanked the entrance to Dreamland, as a schooner with billowing sails and bunting on its rigging ploughed through the waves. Beneath the foam and the keel was a curtain of water through which visitors passed as they slipped into a mysterious underwater realm. Luna Park, on the other hand, was resplendent with feverish electric light, emitted by millions of bulbs, creating a cosmos of luminescence that danced around its fantastic towers so that they looked like silhouettes from another world, a world that could no longer be measured by earthly standards. The flowing current of light cast a spell over visitors to the park—the world over. A critical observer spoke of the "poetry of the electro-technical exhibition," even at a purely technical presentation such as the International Electricity Exhibition in Frankfurt in 1891, which combined two phenomena—water and electricity—in the image of an artificial waterfall. Emil Peschkau was greatly impressed: "The forward motion of a mildly magnetic metal body, attached by wires to cogs, is enough to generate that remarkable level of excitement in the material which is known as electricity … like the vibrations of the particles in water when one throws a stone into it…."[5] Peschkau was quite spellbound by the colorfully lit fountains and water features which looked to him like "red glowing lava," while the female forms emerging from a grotto were bathed in "silver light." This combination of state-of-the-art technology and bombastic imagery was accepted without question, for the public was simply dazzled by the unlimited possibilities of the new technology. And it was exactly this that the amusement parks at Coney Island so successfully gambled on.

The advent of electricity was soon followed by tricks of scale, shrinking larger items to create miniature worlds, which made the visitor seem all the more important, regardless of whether the scenario was a replica of the canals of Venice—which the Venetian Resort in Las Vegas later perfected as a shopping arcade—or Lilliputia, or model trains, or even model steam ships which would engage in miniature sea battles to the amusement of the spectators. In Dreamland, visitors were tossed from destruction to creation, from the Fall of Pompeii to the creation of the world and the Incubator Building, in which newborn babies were saved—again with the aid of the most modern technical means. These amusement parks suggested that civilization had made a huge leap, with electric illuminations and speed as the new metaphors of the modern age, which now even seemed able to conquer the forces of nature, as the public could see in Fighting the Flames, a choreographed inferno fought by heroic firefighters. That the source of the spectators' morbid delight could also become deathly serious became all too clear on May 27, 1911, when

a fire completely destroyed Dreamland, having broken out, as fate would have it, on the Hell Gate Boat Ride. The inferno affected all the parks. In 1907, it was the turn of Steeplechase Park, when the only thing left standing amongst the smoking ruins was Tilyou's logo of a grinning man with thirty-six teeth, looming like a strange *vanitas* figure; it may not even seem too far-fetched to see his grimace as the model for Batman's opponent Joker, the arch-scoundrel, grinning as he spreads fear on all sides. But no fire could halt the unstoppable rise of the amusement park, at least not yet.

A Trip to the Moon

Tilyou's Steeplechase Park was followed by new, even bigger attractions. Inspired by Tilyou's Trip to the Moon, in 1903 the designer Frederic Thompson and his partner, Elmer Dundy, designed a spectacle whose name became known the world over: Luna Park. More than two generations before the first flight to the moon, the masses could already realize their dreams of visiting other worlds. Thompson, who had dropped out of architecture school, was the right man for the job. He was able to channel vague notions of distant worlds and myths of the future à la Jules Verne into a single coherent design. Rem Koolhaas, recognizing his achievement, described him as the "first professional designer active on the island."[6] And as such, he introduced order into the previous cheerfully makeshift nature of the park. His own creation was carefully planned. It was to look different from everything else, captivatingly alien: "As it is a place of amusement, I have eliminated all classical conventional forms from its structure and taken a sort of free renaissance and Oriental type for my model, using spires and minarets wherever I could, in order to get the restive, joyous effect to be derived always from the graceful lines given in this style of architecture."[7]

Thompson's statement set the tone for the future of architecture. This world was not enough; specifically its previously rational architecture was not enough. In the end, Luna Park was illuminated by a good 1.3 million bulbs on 1,326 minarets so that at night it became a magic kingdom of light, a world beyond our own world, designed to do one thing above all: kindle the viewer's imagination. The world of fantasy—so long the sole preserve of the nobility with their pavilions, summer residences, tea houses, and follies; and later the upper middle classes in seaside resorts and villas—was now suddenly accessible to the lowly clerk and factory worker. Thompson fabricated dreams for the masses. And for these he drew his inspiration from the ornaments popular amongst the masses and laid out whole forests of fantastic towers. And there were miniature fleets representing the great seafaring nations; German, Irish, and Inuit villages; and a market place from Delhi: all of which Disney's EPCOT would replicate on a grand scale two generations later. The world as an exotic place where visitors become giants found itself up against parallel worlds—defying the imagination—and technological wonders. Whereas before the Freak Shows were the only places where human beings were put on display, Dr. Couney's Infant Incubator presented premature babies with a chance of survival that was only possible in very few

You can rely on the
Cyclone: the historic site
of this roller coaster is a
magnet for visitors to
Coney Island.

clinics. Luna Park offered visitors a thrill ride into the future, into a romantically transfigured world of speed and technical progress, not even seen previously at World Expositions.
Speculation, fantasy, and optimism all left their mark on an architectural style determined
to free itself from everything that smacked of convention, although it would be true to say
that Frederic Thompson never escaped from the beaux-arts tradition inculcated into him
during his training.

Luna Park set standards that future enterprises had to meet if they wanted to be successful. And their success would be measured against their capacity to correctly gauge
popular taste, as Tilyou had done. As it turned out, State Senator William Reynolds
invested around three million dollars in Dreamland, which was to be greater than anything
the country had ever seen. It had its own pier, 2,625 feet long (800 m) and big enough for
the passenger ferries from Manhattan to drop anchor; 60,000 people could stroll along the
Boardwalk at any one time; and the 260-foot (85.5 m) ramp of Shoot-the-Chutes could
launch two toboggans at a time accommodating 7,000 adventurers per hour, who were
borne aloft in an elevator.

With Coney Island providing ever new variants on modern modes of transport, which
appeared in the guise of entertainment and rides, the real transport question was crucial
from the outset: How were thousands of visitors to be deposited on the outskirts of
Brooklyn? In the mid-1870s, the exclusive hotels were still running their own railroads,
but with the massive bridge-building projects of 1883 —the Brooklyn Bridge—and

1903—the Williamsburg Bridge—traffic at Coney Island positively exploded, more so after 1919 when local transport reached as far as Stillwell Avenue. Coney Island became known as the Nickel Empire because the journey there cost just five cents. While crowds of up to half a million people thronged there on weekends and public holidays in the early twentieth century, by the 1920s the numbers had doubled. Then the Depression hit the country. In 1933, Luna Park was declared bankrupt, and in August 1944, a fire razed to the ground its neglected rides and structures. The gates were closed and it was only after World War II that Coney Island started to rise from the ashes with just one amusement park, the oldest, Steeplechase Park, and other independently run attractions like the Tornado, a roller coaster from 1936. On July 4, 1947, Coney Island welcomed an astounding 1.3 million visitors, one last high point before the pleasure mile started to lose the battle with television and other more exotic holiday destinations. The dilapidated district went downhill, long-established businesses folded, the middle classes moved out to the suburbs, and, on September 20, 1964, Steeplechase Park finally closed. The onetime "Funny Place" had run its course after over sixty years in business. What was it that Thompson once said? "A stationary Luna Park would be an anomaly."[8] Now the Park itself had become an anomaly in an age of air travel and dozens of TV channels from which to choose. Pleasure was now to be had elsewhere.

A National Playground

Coney Island arrived with all the strength of a force of nature, unpredictable and incalculable; it swept human beings along with it and cast a spell over them with its now crude, now sophisticated mixture of attractions and amusements by the beach. "It is blatant, it is cheap, it is the apotheosis of the ridiculous," commented Reginald Wright Kaufman in 1909, and added: "It is like Niagara Falls or the Grand Canyon or Yellowstone Park. It is a

Once the largest amusement park in the United States, Coney Island off-season presents a desolate picture.

Nathan's Famous at the junction of Surf and Stillwell Avenues keeps day-trippers happy with hearty hot dogs.

national playground and not to have seen it is not to have seen our own country."[9] Today, after so many years, the basic layout of the old Coney Island is still recognizable: the promenade by the beach, the Bowery—an alley with traders of every kind in the midst of the amusement business, and the sickle-shaped Surf Avenue which, like a hand opening out towards the sea, separated the residential and business district behind it from the beach and formed the main artery of the pleasure trail. Nowadays Russian advertisements crown huge shop windows and isolated Freak Shows entice visitors. So what does it mean when this urban test bed rusts and disappears? In his wonderful book on Coney Island, John S. Berman offers a likely if sobering assessment of the situation: "Coney Island exemplified the movement away from Victorian refinement and the shaping of a new 'mass culture' in America. The sharp decline . . . can also be seen as emblematic of the decay of New York City and other urban communities."[10] Big business in the entertainment world has long since moved elsewhere, but anyone who goes to Las Vegas can see that Coney Island lives on, simply updating its old dreams: from the Canals of Venice to the Elephant, James Lafferty's hotel built in 1885 in the shape of a vast pachyderm—the prototype for the iconic structure Robert Venturi and Denise Scott Brown later referred to as the "Duck."

What remains? A fresh hot dog, of course, thank to Nathan's Famous Hot Dogs since 1916; and the beach, when it's bathing season and the signs have been taken down with their warnings to visitors: "Beach closed, No Lifeguard on Duty, Swimming prohibited."

The Oktoberfest — What Remains of the Day

Nothing is sadder than the morning after the night before. The party is over; the euphoria has vanished. Crumpled paper cups, lottery tickets, and cigarette butts are strewn across the asphalt where only yesterday hundreds of thousands were making their way to the Augustiner, the Schottenhamel, or the Löwenbräu. The 171st Oktoberfest—the Münchner Wiesn— is over. Clouds race across a fresh, deep blue sky and there is a buzz of activity on the Theresienwiese. A stallholder sweeps together big heaps of trash behind her tent, and men in blue remove litter from the Wiesn. There are cries and quick commands: every minute counts. The first booths have already been loaded up and stand like toys on flatbed trucks; break down teams take plastic figures from the rides and maneuver them up the ramps of the waiting transporters; delivery vans weave their way through the vehicles parked all along the roadway (the Wirtsbudenstrasse) between the abandoned tents. Everywhere there are signs of departure. The octopus arms of the rides droop towards the ground, the roof of the Autoscooter has been taken down, and tinsel dangles from long rods. Only the larger- than-life couple in traditional costumes outside the Ochsenbraterei in Spaten Brewery's tent is still turning a spit as though the fun and games were not over after all. Every few moments the maid lifts up her skirt, revealing a white underskirt for all to see. Frivolity and tradition, abandon and orgies, are as much part of the Oktoberfest as the "goat's beard" on a Bavarian hat or the *lederhosen* which the people of Munich proudly don once a year, just like the beer tankard hats worn by tourists, who walk taller as a result. Locals and visitors alike put on their uniform for the most serious business in the world: having a good time.

By now there are approximately 2,000 Oktoberfest clones—the biggest in the United States, Canada, and Brazil—but there is only one original, with around six million visitors. The Münchner Wiesn, recognized as the largest public festival in the world, is like a meteor that lights up, gleams, and after sixteen days dies down again.

A holy place and time out from normal life: like the Carnival in Venice, a place where— despite the VIP tent and the reserved boxes in the beer halls—brother meets brother on a grand scale. The extra-strength Oktoberfest beer with 13 to 15 percent original wort lowers inhibitions, and the orchestrated coziness, music, and crowded conditions add to an overwhelming feeling of brotherhood. The Oktoberfest is a sanctioned time out of a kind known only in Catholic countries: a time out from order, class, hierarchies, and respectability. An absolutely anarchic energy grips natives, interlopers, and tourists alike. The weak person falls, sins, regrets, and confesses. It is not for nothing that this spectacle, which has taken place annually on the Theresienwiese since October 12, 1810, seems to be a mixture of carnival, harvest festival, and mystery play. With its booths, dummies, and tents the Wiesn provide a stage where costumed visitors can do what they like; some in *lederhosen* or dirndl dresses, others as fanatical orgy-goers with tankard hats.

If you also count the beer gardens, there are sixteen tents with seating for 94,223— a medium-sized town celebrating and swaying arm-in-arm, bawling out songs, and dancing on the tables. Neighborhoods form and dissipate again in a framework of wood and fabric,

Each one of the tents at the Oktoberfest has its own appeal, like the Hippodrome that catches the visitor's eye with its yellow lettering on a red background.

a setting which promises that oneness the beer benches already offer: everyone on the bench sits at the same height at the same long table, drinking beer and moving to the music. To understand it at all, one has to try to imagine these immense tents that make their impact above all by their scale, not by their design. Take the Pschorr-Bräurosl-Festhalle for instance, made from 392 cubic yards (300 m³) of wood and 100 tons of steel. It takes two months of hard labor before all 65,000 square feet (6,000 m²) of cotton fabric have been hung from the roof. Then at last the tent—262 feet long by 197 feet wide by 44 feet high (80 x 60 x 13.5 m)—is ready to receive visitors from all over the world. New records are constantly being set at the Wiesn. Everything is bigger here, from the giant pretzels to the insignias of the breweries, and in the form of larger-than-life figures at the Löwenbräu, for instance. The heraldic Bavarian lion, on a column next to the tent, grasps a jug of beer in its paw and opens its jaws wide to savor the cool liquid with its stylized frothing head.

By contrast, in the Augustiner-Festhalle, two tents away, there are so-called "deer," 200-liter wooden barrels from which the Oktoberfest beer is tapped. The logistics behind the tents is equally impressive: in the Hofbräu-Festzelt, 300 employees serve up to 11,000 guests, and the Ochsenbraterei roasts 1,500-pound (680 kg) steers for six to seven hours until the colossal beasts, divided into 700 portions, end up on the guests' plates. A concession to sell beer is an investment that has to be very carefully calculated. "The cost of erecting a tent plus the rent for the pitch costs around 1.6 million euros,"[11] explains Toni Roiderer, spokesman for the Oktoberfest landlords.

Beer tents bring people
together: everyone is the
same when sitting on a
bench.

A Royal Spectacle

It all started with a wedding, a royal spectacle. After celebrations
lasting five days to commemorate the marriage of Crown Prince
Ludwig of Bavaria and Therese von Sachsen-Hildburghausen,
on October 17, 1810, the old "Scarlet Race"—a horse race—
was revived. It was such a success that it was repeated the
following year. Since then the Wiesn has become the festival to
end all festivals thanks to attractions such as the "Steckerlfisch
und Krinoline" carousel, or the Schichtl founded in 1871, which
advertises itself as the "original magic specialty theater" and
proudly presents the "beheading of a living person by means of
a guillotine." The Wiesn attractions have always reflected the
development of the modern entertainment industry—faster,
higher, further.

When, in 1908, the Schottenhamel became the first of the
great beer tents to boast electric lighting, it was greeted as
something very special. Nowadays, the Löwenbräu tent is illuminated by 16,500 bulbs. In the evening, the Wiesn is filled
with rotating lamps and vast illuminations. The rides turn the
largest public festival in the world into a magical place of light
and adventure, completely out of proportion to its material reality. It seems as though the pirouettes of the octopuses and the
convolutions of the roller coaster enter a new dimension, which
William Turner long ago identified as the incarnation of modernity. Space, light, and time become "spacelighttime," where
the movements of the masses leave traces in the air, and the
people cavort far beyond the simple wooden booths, steaming
tents, rigging, and containers. The joyful loss of control is very
much part of the amusement park experience, and even more
so part of the Oktoberfest. The visitors dull their coordination
skills and perceptive faculties with alcohol, they dress up and
go on rides that spin them through space like human projec-
tiles, and they move in an architectural scenario with flying
structures that are utterly solid in their construction yet create
the impression of fleeting transience — all the more so than in a
permanent amusement park. Anything can happen here; this is a
place where the only limitations are set by one's own powers of
imagination, a place that dissolves each evening into light and
sound that blurs boundaries and invites us to overstep them.

You can always rely on the Eurostar, the roller coaster that
has been the main attraction at the Oktoberfest since 1995. Get
in! Get in! Spectacles, cell phones, cameras, and any other loose
objects have to be handed in. The attendant is already pressing
the safety bars down; yellow half-belts click into position. In the
inverted coaster, the passengers don't travel on a track, but
dangle instead in their hard-shell seats, locked in with a shoulder
brace. One signal, and a chain-lift raises the twenty-eight passengers into the air. Nearly 100 feet (30 m) above the ground

the train comes to a rest, and then the Eurostar plunges earthward. At a speed of 50 miles (81 km) per hour, the passengers hurtle into the first loop. Stomachs lurch. At the highest point of the 85-foot-high (26 m) parabolic curve the world stands on its head, your legs fly upwards, and then the vehicle speeds up again towards the ground. Still a good 2,600 feet (800 m) to go; a zero-gravity roll with integrated heartline spin—the so-called revolution—and two corkscrews: an eternity, until after just forty-six seconds the fun is over.

Why do people find it so fascinating to turn the world upside down? Why do they love to be intoxicated by speed? Eugen Roth has described the roller coaster as a "source of sensual delight and fear," thereby pre-empting the psychologists' evaluation. In the ordered world of modernity, occupied by office workers with life and third party insurance, there is evidently an increasing hunger for marginal experiences, for bungee jumping and canyoning as a way of proving to oneself that one is still fully alive.

Quick to put up and quick to take down: the architecture at the Oktoberfest has to be one thing at least—mobile.

Let us make no mistake, mass entertainment is thoroughly rational in its organization. Logistics determine the nature of the fun, as is nowhere more evident than in the temporary town of tents and booths, restocked each morning with fresh supplies to be consumed during the course of the day. From a bird's-eye-view, the Theresienwiese looks like an oversized liver in an otherwise built-up area, and the ordered layout of the streets intersecting below the Bavaria make the site look more like a Roman camp than a gigantic tented fairground. The site is split asymmetrically by Matthias-Pschorr-Strasse. The smaller part to the left is given over to the Bayerische Zentral-Landwirtschaftsfest, an agricultural fair. The Wiesn itself actually consists of the sixteen beer tents along the Wirtsbudenstrasse in the northern part, with the rides on either side of the Schaustellerstrasse in the southern part. None of the other connecting routes has a proper name; they are just numbered streets, one to four, as in a new town that has not taken the trouble to immortalize its pioneers. The reason is rather mundane. Once the Oktoberfest is over, these routes disappear into the green grass, and all that remains are the posters at the nearby metro station and the Wiesn souvenirs on the shelves at the tourist information center.

1 Rem Koolhaas, *Delirious New York: A Retroactive Manifesto for Manhattan* (New York, 1994), p. 30.
2 John S. Berman, *Coney Island* (New York, 2003), p. 15.
3 Even the *New York Times* described the grubbier end of the beach resort "Sodom-by-the-Sea." Ibid., p. 17.
4 Berman, *Coney Island*, p. 16.
5 Emil Peschkau, "Die Poesie der Elektrotechnischen Ausstellung," in *Gartenlaube*, 1891, pp. 637 and 640. As quoted in *Kristallisationen, Splitterungen: Bruno Tauts Glashaus* (Basel, 1993), pp. 36–7.
6 Koolhaas, *Delirious New York*, p. 38.
7 Ibid., p. 39.
8 "The Annual Awakening of the Only Coney Island," *New York Times*, May 6, 1906. As quoted in Koolhaas, *Delirious New York*, p. 41.
9 Berman, *Coney Island*, p. 9.
10 Ibid.
11 *Süddeutsche Zeitung*, no. 258, November 6–7, 2004, p. 51.

DISNEY WORLD

The Power of Perfection

"Have you noticed?" asks the friendly manager, "everything's off kilter here." And it's true, sloping surfaces wherever you look. Not a single stretch of horizontal concrete; rather gentle slopes, little hills and valleys, and raised centerlines. "Because of the rain," says the Disney man, "it can really pour here." Rain? EPCOT (Experimental Prototype Community of Tomorrow) lies under a leaden sky, not a breath of wind disturbs the carefully cultivated borders, reddish-brown concrete slabs that look as though they had been laid for the Queen of England herself—here anyone who can endure the sloping concrete ground feels that they are King or Queen of the park. Surfaces slope as though they were laid on purpose to adjust the visitor's gaze; a displacement of the usual axes that occurs spontaneously as you approach Disney World on pathways that dislocate everyday life, making it slip and slide, turning it upside down. First, the colors change. Street signs turn into bright signals with jolly lines painted in fresh hues. The "one way" sign is fixed to a mint-colored pole, crowned by a blue top hat with three yellow lines. Everything is privately owned here since the company bought up 43 square miles (110 km^2) of central Florida in the 1960s for six million dollars and turned it into the largest amusement park in the world. Next, the shapes change. The grass at the Walt Disney World Resort is dense, the roads curve through a subtropical landscape where movement is fun. As Walt Disney remarked in 1966 in his last film, made just a month before his death, Orlando is strategically placed in the heart of the Sunshine State: "In fact, we've selected this site because it's so easy for tourists and Florida residents to get here by automobile." The film shows Disney standing surrounded by plans and maps, evidently in the workshop where dreams are made. With a pointer he gestures towards Central Florida, half general, half geography teacher: "Disney World is located just a few miles from the crossing point of Interstate 4 and Sunshine State Parkway, Florida's major highways carrying motorists east and west and north and south through the center of the state."[1]

And then there is the parking lot in front of EPCOT, a huge asphalt fan in the landscape, each section in perfect order. The attendants wave you in and smile as they do so. Here it is clear that everything is about logistics. "People and vehicles are constantly

previous double pages: Spaceship Earth with Mickey, the sorcerers's apprentice who provides the geodetic sphere added luster.

The visionary Walt Disney and his own dream come true.

in motion at Disneyland,"[2] says the voiceover, and he's right. As soon as you have
passed the ticket booths, you have to start walking. Not a stroll but an extended hike,
a profoundly un-American experience that the monorail, intermittently whizzing by,
seems to openly mock. The elevated monorail track connects Magic Kingdom Park with
EPCOT, and as it swishes along it seems to be issuing some kind of a threat: sore feet,
blisters, and calluses. In a streamlined vehicle high above the visitors' head you can
see it passing by—the spirit of utopia, the optimism of the space age which was to
lead Walt Disney to ignite the next stage of his entertainment universe (though he was
never to see it for himself), just an hour's drive away from Cape Canaveral's space
center. In 1971—half a decade after Disney's death—Disney World was opened in
Orlando, a hundred times bigger than Disneyland in Anaheim, California, which opened
in 1955 and is the father of all Disney parks. Little is left of the utopian futurist settlement other than a constantly evolving dream world, which is constantly putting out
new branches into the steaming subtropical forest of Florida, in the form of attractions
such as Disney MGM Studios, Disney's Blizzard Beach Water Park, Disney's Typhoon
Lagoon, Downtown Disney, and Disney's Animal Kingdom. A visit to just one of the
Fab Four—Magic Kingdom Park, EPCOT, Disney MGM Studios, or Animal Kingdom—
takes at least a day, for in his dream worlds Disney had also been experimenting with
deceleration.

Memorial stones next to the monorail? Not at all! The granite steles bear inscriptions from satisfied visitors.

Retrodesign for Futuristic visions

While Walt Disney still had an eye on Coney Island when he was developing Disneyland and—with the rigor of a screenwriter and the magic of his own cartoon characters—turned the familiar features of an amusement park into his own dream world with retro designs and gleaming futuristic visions—protected by a 20-foot-high (6 m) earthen dyke to prevent the illusion from being shattered—the sheer size of Disney World meant that it was unthreatened by its surroundings. With Disney World, the company perfected the amusement park with an array of sub-worlds (Magic Kingdom alone has four: Adventureland, Fantasyland, Frontierland, and Tomorrowland; all connected by Main Street USA) and made the leap to the all-around marketing of its leisure product. Family-friendly fun à la Disney ranges from the lollipop at a stand to the hamburger in the restaurant to the hotel room in the company-owned accommodation. On a site twice the size of Manhattan the Walt Disney World Resort is able to exploit every link in the chain of the leisure industry. Its size means that it has no competition. The freeriders who profited from the smaller size of the Californian park are kept at arm's-length in the heart of Florida, if not actually shaken off. Disney World is not designed for once-in-a-lifetime visits. It encourages visitors to come again and again, with their children and then grandchildren. Here everyone is part of one big happy family, the Disney family. And, as such, visitors to EPCOT can have themselves immortalized with their picture on a granite stele near the entrance to the park.

As part of the "Leave a Legacy" scheme, dozens of visitors have had a photograph of themselves engraved into the granite, a special gift from the operators to all those who have taken advantage of the Dream Maker Package and stayed in an original Disney Resort hotel. This total identification with the park gives the visitors a role in the entertainment, as the decorative images of a huge family. The field of steles next to the 177-foot-high (54 m) Spaceship Earth inspired by Buckminster Fuller, looks—well it does—like a socialist cemetery for heroic cosmonauts who never returned from their voyages to the stars. And above them flashes the geodesic dome with its Mickey Mouse hand showering sparks from a wand—glittering sequins over a sweltering amusement park.

Imagineering: a Blending of Creative Imaginations with Technical Know-How

As in all dream worlds, crucial importance is given to the transition between outside and inside, the barrier that has to be overcome before one can at last enter and become part of it all. EPCOT's entrance is in effect a huge engine that shovels people in, speeds them up, and spits them out again behind Spaceship Earth, leaving them to disperse into the pavilions laid out in a semicircle or to make their way to the World Showcase in the next area. From a bird's-eye view, the layout is very clear. First, there is the convex line of ticket booths and security checks. Once visitors have passed these they plunge into a cone-shaped space with the geodesic sphere, Spaceship Earth, at its narrowest point. Behind that is an ellipse-shaped area flanked by pavilions like two open hands. Directly ahead of the visitor, invitingly lies the lake with the national pavilions. Spaceship Earth is the main attraction. If there is already a line, visitors might walk by and try again on the way back. No other structure can rival the silvery golf ball, which can be seen from miles away, proudly dominating the flat landscape. The sphere fulfils the function of the castle in the

A miniature Paris complete with the Eiffel Tower.

A piece of China within arm's reach: it's simply a matter of scale.

A piece of China within arm's reach: it's simply a matter of scale.

classical Magic Kingdom, it centers the visitors' gaze as the monorail whizzes above their heads.

The architecture of EPCOT is iconographic, it recreates and reinforces pictorial worlds taken from the storyboard of movie productions. These form a backdrop that sets in motion desires and ideas which are brought to life by means of Audio-Animatronics and specifically designed landscapes. The process itself makes no detours or intellectual references. Architecture is part of a story that is planned with the same degree of attention a director would give to a new movie. It is both a medium for dreams and the ever-elastic putty that holds together individual pictures.

In the World Showcase, a permanent World Exposition of sorts, these pictures have become clichés, drawing on the most obvious associations: China—a round temple based on the design of the Temple of Heaven in Beijing; Paris—culinary delights with Paul Bocuse in twisting alleys; Germany—a mixture of all different kinds of *Fachwerk* houses and separate towns. The typical is joined with the symbolic to become the signifier. "All elements are brought together in a limited space by a masterly manipulation of scale and proportion that produces a sense of magnificent sizes and distances,"[3] to quote the historian Elting E. Morison on EPCOT's historical panoramas which are in themselves prototypical of the techniques of representation used by Disney. History and stories eddy and swirl in one huge playground for young and old. The journey through eleven different countries in around eighty minutes takes up one part of the park; the other part contains

the more ambitious Future World, with its pavilions bringing together all the utopian movie sets of recent decades, which could hold their own with any Bond movie. While in the movies only miscreants live in a sphere which debilitates the familiar and, amalgamating the old and the new, exposes it, here everyone can go on a Journey Into Imagination and walk on glass Mayan pyramids and discover that they are merely decorative props or— as in the case of the curved Living Seas Pavilion constructed in the mid-1980s—find that it is simply a skillfully disguised ramp with twisting curves designed solely to absorb and slow up the flood of visitors. The structure itself is dug into a hillside and looks like a wave retreating from a beach, leaving behind a disintegrating sandcastle with smoothed-out edges and softened forms. All the more astonishing is the flowing entrance area— a vivid relief of an ocean and a picture-book sunset. And then there is the Mission: Space Pavilion, which seems to be absolutely bursting with energy, pouring the centrifugal force of the rotating system of planets into an elliptical spatial curve. Space travel to Mars is anticipated in the sculptural centrifuge of the outer skin. Disney deploys movie sequences and film stills to give an impression today of what the adventures of tomorrow will be like, even to the extent of the hard, crystalline nature of the Universe of Energy Pavilion sponsored by ExxonMobil. This cube, clad in mirrored tiles and brushed aluminum, has 80,000 solar cells on its roof. Form and content perfectly match and reinforce each other, and the iconography as a whole uses symbols and the replication of themes to give a tangible sense of the attractions yet to come.

If anywhere, there has to be a sense of utopia in the drama of the sweeping ornament of The Living Seas, with its stylized sunrise floating above the exhibition like a portent of a better new world.

The Value of a Coherent Vision

It seems that the world is nothing more than the will to imagine, and this will has rarely been so perfectly realized as by Disney, who understood the value of a coherent vision; above all a vision that is continuous and open to further development. In the early days, nine handpicked staff members—the Imagineering Department—watched over the activities of the well-known cartoon characters. Imagineering—a combination of "imagination" and "engineering"—holds the key to the whole of Disney World: guaranteed quality control for all its products and uniform design guidelines for dream(er)s, a unique symbiosis of creativity and rational planning, with a healthy dose of the spirit of the pragmatic engineer: "To plan Disneyland Walt Disney long ago established a design organization called WED Enterprises," we are told by the voiceover in the last Disney film, "today the staff at WED includes designers, architects, and engineers skilled in the 'Disney way.' And also fine craftsmen and technicians skilled in the arts of the space age. What WED does is called Imagineering: a blending of creative imaginations with technical know-how."[4] And psychology, he might have added. Disney's strategy of prettifying relies on fun facades behind which lie cubic dream stores, subterranean service tunnels, and ducts. Of course, the visitor sees none of this. On Main Street reality shrinks to five-eighths its normal size; things look sweet, consumable, and universal. The Strip Mall, with its candy and souvenir shops, is designed so that everyone feels big, yet sheltered, in this homey, harmless atmosphere

of yesteryear—a time Walt Disney decided to celebrate in 1955 when all over the United States the livelihoods of small retailers and the friendly folk on Main Street were threatened with extinction by the devastating arrival of automotive mobility. A day in Paradise—guaranteed to be friendly and stress-free.

There are no bits of paper lying around, no gum spat out onto the ground, and certainly no cigarette butts as you would see in European amusement parks—despite the presence of millions of visitors every year.[5] Disney lives by its perfect organization; the parks celebrate cleanliness and order as the highest virtues. Perfect hygiene distinguishes

A typical, timeless medieval scene, condensed into an accumulation of roofs, turrets, and gables. Years later Las Vegas will perfect this same illusion with New York New York.

these sites. Even the cleaning personnel wear white as though they were working in an operating room. Above all, Disney's world is timeless. Pictures of decay simply don't exist, as garbage trucks could destroy this harmonious world. Garbage is removed below ground through the Magic Kingdom's 1.4 miles (2.2 km) of subterranean service tunnels, which the professionally friendly staff also uses for shift changes. And some of this discipline seems to brush off on the visitors, who wait patiently in line with the understanding that the lines outside the various attractions are part of the bigger picture. Even fun has to be disciplined and regulated; how else could it be that on the Internet, standing in line is referred to as an important part of the impression left by a visit to Disneyland? One tourist from overseas, for instance, writes: "But after just 45 minutes in the entertainingly fitted-out waiting area it's already our turn and we love the ride. Test Track is one of the best rides I've ever been on in a theme park."[6] Another visitor advises us to arrive early to secure the best seats for the fireworks and laser show staged every evening.

A World of Its Own

In this leisure world, Disney is its own master. In return for some tens of thousands of new jobs, Florida generously granted the company the rights of a municipal body. Operating as the Reedy Creek Improvement District, it has its own highway construction department and police force. No wonder Walt Disney described this project as "the most exciting and challenging assignment we've ever tackled at Walt Disney Productions."[7] Even if only a part of the astonishing plans were realized— EPCOT is only a faint reflection of the planned city of the future—and without some of the intended key features such as the Airport of the Future, control is still the watchword at every level, affecting the scale, transportation routes, and even the history, which is condensed, in the Disney manner, into a few minutes in Spaceship Earth.

Naturally, in the "land far, far away" (as Disneyland is known to aficionados), questions are also raised concerning the laws of artificiality. Travel guides are forever alluding to the "artificial" atmosphere at Disney World and commenting, with a malicious sneer, that the only real things are the sets visitors see at the backstage tour at Disney MGM Studios because "authenticity is a rarity in the Walt Disney World."[8] Elsewhere writers describe it as a "funny fake world,"[9] a "pretend world,"[10] although it had admittedly been created "with the greatest attention to detail" and is an "outstanding reconstruction," while rides in other parks are "technically outdated amusements" which "would be better in a fairytale park."[11] Even more important than the self-evident fact that Disney World is only authentic with regard to its own precepts—the Disney universe—and not to the world familiar to the visitors (why else should they come?), is the fact that Disney creates worlds, it does not copy them. These worlds, cinematic compositions created according to a storyboard, in turn generate their own reality by presenting fully coherent concepts. Every detail is intrinsic to the whole, down to the specially designed garbage cans and emblems. These are as important to Disney as the overall form; the right feeling matters as much as the scale and the colors, which draw attention to different activities in spotlight zones. Disney's worlds are more than just perfect sets, they are interactive scenarios where spectators become actors, meet real characters in a three-dimensional comic-strip world, and take snapshots of these moments back home with them.

Tomorrow's Dream World

Disney's unique combination of technology and dreams—which the company also displayed to the public away from the park at the New York World's Fair in 1964 and 1965[12]—was keenly observed by professionals in the field. Town planner James W. Rouse was more than fulsome in his praise at the Urban Design Conference at Harvard University in 1963: "I hold a view that may be somewhat shocking to an audience as sophisticated as this: that the greatest piece of urban design in the United States today is Disneyland."[13] Three years later, Walt Disney embarked on what was to be his greatest coup, not only presenting tomorrow's world as a gaily-colored dreamland, but also making a serious attempt to face up to the problems society would face in the future.

What should our lives look like in the future? This question preoccupied Walt Disney all his life and he came up with an ambitious answer: EPCOT, a model project for 20,000 residents taking advantage of the latest technical advances. Major American corporations were to co-finance the project, thereby introducing a wider public to their visionary thinking: urban marketing of the kind that well-meaning industrialists had already been propagating since the turn of the century. The town of the future would be laid out like rays, promised

The last frontier — the Mission: SPACE Pavilion extends dramatically and becomes a space station for astronauts.

the company that knew how to make dreams come true. At the heart of the town would be the community center, "accessible from all the residential areas without the need for transport."[14] A town that has much about it of that time's obsession with mega-structures and radial layouts, as proposed by Archigram, amongst others. EPCOT is a child of its time, nurtured on the prevalent faith in unlimited growth—if necessary on the seabed, on the moon, or even somewhere in space. A concept drawing shows this "town of the future" not in sunny Florida, but in the north, with conifers and cold blue colors, out of which the center glows with dazzling brightness, answered by a matching tower on the horizon—the

next settlement built upon exactly the same principle, with dwellings around a gigantic center that controls everything like a spider.

Disney found his inspiration for this organic structure not only in the history of the ideal town but also right on his own doorstep, as it were, at the World's Fair in New York in 1939, with its national pavilions and, above all, with its sites where American corporations presented the latest technological advances and their possible impact on everyday life. Disney, however, a promoter through and through, mingled the profane with the heroic and business acumen with thoughts of the frontier, which also exist here in Florida.

A New Frontier

"EPCOT will take its cue from the new ideas and new technologies that are now emerging from the creative centers of American industry. It will be a community of tomorrow that will never be completed, but will always be introducing, and testing, and demonstrating new materials and new systems. And EPCOT will always be a showcase to the world of the ingenuity and imagination of American free enterprise. I don't believe there is a challenge anywhere in the world that's more important to people everywhere than finding solutions to the problems of our cities."[15] Clearly, this was much more than just a continuation of the nostalgic approach that had been behind Disney's idealization of Main Street in his Californian theme park, created at a time when the small towns of his childhood were perishing with the then new dominance of the automobile. Here it is as though Walt Disney were creating a legacy for future generations, a futuristic design to help solve the problems inherent in the city. And he speaks of a time which, perfectly naturally, will talk of freedom and progress in the same breath, which could even combine them as the basis of a great ideology of constant growth.

However, with Disney's death in 1966, his high-flying plans were shattered. A whole era was unraveling. The Space Age was about to reach its climax, and the impending oil crisis was to demonstrate for the first time that there were limits to growth. EPCOT opened in 1982, a 1.2-billion-dollar theme park boasting the latest technology that included a permanent world's fair, the so-called World Showcase. This exhibition—constructed around a geodesic sphere and formerly known as Future World, focusing on the future of, amongst other things, energy production, communications, agriculture, and transportation—was to become one thing above all—a showcase for American industry, exactly as Walt Disney had wanted it: "We don't presume to know all the answers. In fact, we're counting on the cooperation of American industry to provide their very best thinking during the planning and the creation of our Experimental Prototype Community of Tomorrow. And most important of all, when EPCOT has become a reality and we find the need for technologies that don't even exist today, it's our hope that EPCOT will stimulate American industry to develop new solutions that will meet the needs of people expressed right here in this experimental community."[16] Companies like AT&T, Exxon, and General Motors invested millions in pavilions of their own. Others, like Kodak, drew on Disney's know-how to make their presentations entertaining; Coca-Cola offered refreshments and samples of food from all over the world. Progress was presented as the preserve of major corporations—an extremely disturbing notion today.

Organization is paramount: Disney even sets up the perfect snapshot.

In The Land Pavilion it is always Sunshine Season.

Life in Dreamland

Power and glory: the Dolphin is more than generous in its dimensions.

A walk through Disney World is like a guided tour through a sociological laboratory, where all the wishes and needs of the visitors are considered in advance and translated into an architectural dressing. Disney's integrated concept covers the staff, the buildings, and their decoration, all of which are carefully matched. Clean and family-friendly; safe and well-tested. Since Disney parks were to be free of problems or cares, even signs prohibiting certain activities were disguised as polite reminders. Problems? They have to stay

outside; they have no business here. Enjoy and relax is the motto. Once the visitors have paid their admission fee, they are free to enjoy all the attractions, even though they have to stand in line for them. Disney parks are designed to foster perfect delight, and the staff does everything in their power to see that that is how it stays. By the mid-1980s, there were already 18,000 Disney employees in Florida. Since then, besides the five-star mega hotel-resorts Walt Disney World Swan (758 rooms), Walt Disney World Dolphin (1,514 rooms), and Disney's Yacht Resort (630 rooms), around another ten complexes to suit every budget have been added. Hotel guests, who benefit from the "Extra Magic Hour," are allowed into the parks—located at a walking distance from the hotels—an hour before the crowds. The twin hotels, the Swan and the Dolphin, marked the beginning of a new era for Disney embodied in the collaboration between Michael Eisner, since September 1984 the CEO at Disney, and leading architects of the postmodern age, most notably Michael Graves. At one point Michael Graves, Alan Lapidus, and Robert Venturi were in competition with each other, and Graves broke all the unwritten laws that had hitherto defined Disney architecture. The main point is "never to distract the guests' attention unintentionally,"[17] as Beth Dunlop put it. The two mega-structures—costing 225 and 120 million dollars—are visible from everywhere, particu-larly the twenty-seven-story Dolphin. The symbolic creatures on the roofs of these mega-resorts are alone five stories high. The design philosophy behind these symbols is as simple as it is appropriate: "I wanted to do something that a child could iden-tify with but wasn't sappy,"[18] says Graves, whose inspiration cites, amongst other things, garden sculptures and Gian Lorenzo Bernini. These two hotels (1989 and 1990) by the lake—water is still the key element in all Disney theme parks —mark the end of the utterly uncontroversial, perfect cartoon world and the onset of an architectural style that is celebrated by some and mercilessly derided by others.

With the arrival of the architects also came the question: what typifies the Mouse? What should Disney architecture look like? Robert Stern, Arata Isozaki, and—once again—Michael Graves were to come up with the answers. Never had building and the cartoon world been closer, never before had the two-dimensional been transported into a third dimension in a more abstract or more literal way. With stylized Mickey Mouse ears

and direct borrowings, such as the living door handles from
Alice in Wonderland, a whole new wonderland of construction
opened up. Disney acquired variety without appearing arbi-
trary. In a certain sense, the postmodernism of the Disney
school, a child of the spirit of the speech balloon, was on the
point of falling apart. Paul Goldberger, architecture critic of
the *New York Times*, praised Isozaki's Team Building as an
"extraordinary composition."[19]

But the new buildings also raised questions as to the
sociological dimension of Disney World. What is it like to be
a tourist in this perfect holiday world, which you don't have
to even leave at the official closing time, when you simply
transfer from the Disney Park to the Disney hotel? And how
do such huge, iconic buildings of that size fit into the landscape of the park itself? In order to prevent conflicts arising
between different experiences, there are neutral zones—
distance markers like borders, flowerbeds, and lakes. An
extensive network of waterways—which visitors can use to
be shipped from one attraction to the next, or just to recover
and rest by—also fulfills the same task. The storyboard
has grown. The theme park is structured around a single
thematic line, which is taken up and reflected in individual
subsidiary worlds. The Swan and the Dolphin fit into the
existing infrastructure and extend it. Different aspects of
the park are constantly being renovated and regrouped;
elsewhere work is underway on innovations and new features,
which is not to say that the familiar, trusty friends are in
any sense neglected. Disney parks are continually testing out
the dividing line between innovation and preservation, with
a general tendency towards the conservative. Thus visitors
are enticed into the park and encouraged to make return
visits until they completely identify with it: the motives
themselves are, in the true Disney manner, unique and
unmistakable, although usually no more than variations on
a theme. Even paradise has its routines and no one understands that better than Disney.

First, We Take Japan ...

In a homogenized world, where people are ever closer, laughing at the same soap operas, and unpacking the same products, it is all the more astonishing that entertainment is not
yet similarly ubiquitous. In 1983, Disney arrived in Japan;
in 1992, Disneyland Resort Paris was opened in Europe.
However, up until now the offshoot in Marne-la-Vallée near
Paris has not fulfilled the high expectations of its investors.
In 2002, the Film Studio Park opened, costing over 700
million dollars. Far from the anticipated four million visitors,

The perfect boardwalk for
the guests at the resort.

only two million have visited the Film Studio Park to date, "while the first and older theme park has seen a reduction of exactly the same amount in its visitor numbers."[20] All the same, with twelve million visitors per year, Disneyland Resort Paris has become Europe's leading tourist destination. And the dream goes on. Following the construction of the second theme park, work is now underway on an ideal town around the theme park: Val d'Europe, a settlement for 40,000 people, scheduled for completion in 2020. It will take the form of a ring road with a diameter of 1.9 miles (3 km); 7.7 square miles (20 km^2) for development with seven giant hotels with 7,000 rooms, golf courses, and artificial lakes. "In the future each town will have its own 'fairy kingdom' where the citizens will find everything they need" promised a Disney children's book as far back as 1970, "Parklands, lakes, and small rivers will take care of the people's need for rest and relaxation near the town."[21] This is precisely what is happening east of Paris. The Place d'Ariane, in the center of Val d'Europe, has a 0.6-mile-long (1 km) shopping mall, a factory outlet center, and two stations where forty TGV trains from all over Europe stop each day.

In California, at the furthest end of the frontier in terms of both geography and time, Walt Disney realized a deeply American dream, the pursuit of happiness. Many have copied him. The meticulous storyboard, the precisely calculated self-promotion, and the perfect marketing have all paid off. Worldwide the Disney brand stands for having fun and a good time. Disney guarantees clean entertainment for the whole family, and each year the corporation provides readymade entertainment for twenty million visitors and envelops them in an imaginative, three-dimensional fantasy world. Even if not all of its rivals achieve the opulence and rigorous perfection of Disney's details, the dream has taken hold. Nowadays the area southwest of Orlando has become one huge amusement park, with giants that have invested similar sums and have cherry-picked particular segments of the entertainment world—usually with a lot of water and surrounded by a host of smaller attractions that have attached themselves like scavenger fish following a whale, living from its leftovers. International Drive, full of hotels and restaurants, has its own miniature golf courses with erupting volcanoes and floodlights operating until the wee hours. Clones of clones of clones proliferate across the landscape and are turning Orlando into the dream world of the western hemisphere. The Disneyfication of central Florida is an extension of the Coney Island phenomenon where around the amusement park smaller attractions sprang up and withered away again.[22] Only here it is on a gigantic scale. Anyone opening one of the relevant travel brochures has a problem. Which park? And what will I be missing if I only have a week? They are called Busch Gardens, Discovery Grove, Islands of Adventure, Universal Studios, Sea World Adventure Park, or Wet'n'Wild, and they cover everything that comes under the heading "fun for the whole family," with, in addition, the very latest roller coasters, Hollywood figures, and merchandising outlets. You just have to believe the publicity and look forward to the moment when the Killer Whale Shamu "will guaranteed soak you." In the meantime, Orlando has become a magnet for the entertainment industry, attracting ever more players. And as each arrives, the boundaries blur further still. The park becomes a world, and the world a park that doesn't end outside the ticket booths, not even when you sink into your hotel bed at night and zap through the cable TV channels, where you will without a doubt find a feature about the latest, fabulous attraction. Only when you have returned your rental car at the airport and wonder if you remembered to pack your toothbrush does one dream world replace the other. But the park is still whirring and flashing in your head, as you walk past the miles of shops on the way to the gate. Cory Doctorow was right: "The most striking thing about cunning artifice is its sudden absence." Except that that doesn't happen any more—Disneyland is everywhere.

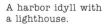

A harbor idyll with a lighthouse.

1 www.waltopia.com/florida_film.html

2 Ibid.

3 Beth Dunlop, *Building a Dream: The Art of Disney Architecture*, with a foreword by Vincent Scully (New York, 1996), p. 59.

4 See note 1 above.

5 Top visitor numbers per day at Magic Kingdom: 10,000 when it was opened in 1971, in 1999 it was around 100,000 for all the parks at Disney World. Fred W. Wright, "Micky wird's schon richten," *Geo Special Florida*, June 13, 1984: 84–94, p. 93. Samantha Cook, *USA—the Rough Guide* (London, 2004). Mick Sinclair, *Florida—the Rough Guide* (London, 1996).

6 "Epcot Center in Disney World: Heute verbringen wir den ganzen Tag im Epcot Center." www.100tage.de/reise/apr18.htm

7 See note 1 above.

8 Samantha Cook, *USA—the Rough Guide* (London, 2004). Mick Sinclair, *Florida—the Rough Guide* (London, 1996).

9 Wright, "Micky wird's schon richten," p. 90.

10 Ibid., p. 92.

11 Ibid., p. 90.

12 "The talents of WED have gone to work outside Disneyland, too. At the New York World's Fair, four of the most popular attractions were Disney shows and corporate exhibits that skillfully welcomed and entertained more than 150,000 people every day." Ibid.

13 Ibid.

14 Von der Steinzeithöhle zum Wolkenkratzer: Walt Disney Enzyklopädie Band 1 (Stuttgart, Ehapa, 1971).

15 See note 1 above and Dunlop, *Building a Dream*, p. 193.

16 Ibid.

17 Dunlop, *Building a Dream*, p. 66.

18 Ibid., p. 70.

19 Ibid., p. 97.

20 Michael Mönninger, "The show has to go on. Euro Disney is deep in debt. But the leisure park outside Paris is so huge that France cannot afford to let it be declared bankrupt." *Die Zeit*, 10/2004.

21 See note 15 above.

22 John S. Berman, *Coney Island* (New York, 2003), p. 66.

LAS VEGAS

The First Mediafied Dream World

"Rental car return?" The woman behind the cash desk looks up briefly as she runs the credit card through the machine. She's in her mid-forties, dyed strands of hair poke out from under her blue baseball cap. "Left across Las Vegas Boulevard, then first left onto Sunset and right onto Bermuda." And because she isn't too busy at the moment she takes a Western Pacific Kraft bag and writes down the directions on it: "Left L.V. Blvd; Left Sunset; Right Bermuda." It reads like a knowing invitation to lose oneself in what Tom Wolfe described as "The Versailles of Pop Culture." Lost in Las Vegas, something Jean Baudrillard dreamed about: "To vanish, in the middle of a motel, in one or other of Nevada's gambling halls."[1]

previous double pages:
This historic sign marks
the beginning of the world-
famous Las Vegas Strip.

Everyday life comes with a bang: lines at the check-in counter, endless waiting, and security checks. There is nothing about this airport different from any other mass transportation building—with a single exception: up until final boarding you can hear the slot machines ringing in an environment of air conditioning and tinted glass. A last-minute gamble before the most successful American creation of the twentieth century melts like butter in the sun of the Nevada desert: streets, junctions, condominiums, warehouses, endless highways, and dormitory suburbs stretch as far as the horizon. The greater Las Vegas area, which includes downtown Las Vegas, Henderson, North Las Vegas, and Boulder City, has a population of one and a half million, almost six times as large as in 1970. In addition, there are the thirty million visitors who leave billions of dollars behind them in the casinos and guarantee hotel occupancy rates of around 85 percent. Las Vegas, which has transformed itself from a pit of vice into a destination for family vacations, is at the top of the list of tourist attractions, ahead of New York City or Paris, whose own silhouettes gleam along the Strip like the windows of a boutique.

If America is movement, then Las Vegas is permanent acceleration. The Boulevard revolves to the rhythm of roulette wheels, computer gaming, and one-arm bandits; even the architecture vibrates in the glow of millions of light bulbs that transform facades into signs and surfaces into moving pictures. Las Vegas is like a vast *tableau vivant*, an installation piece on the American Way of Life, fast-paced and always on the go, a place, with its gaze firmly concentrated on maximizing profit, that constantly reinvents itself. Architecture functions here as a container for histories and a shell that can be remodeled at any time to suit the performances offered by the entertainment industry. Stage sets, theaters, and

The rear view of Las Vegas Boulevard still
reveals the sediments of its history of success:
repositories, memories of the old Strip, and the
expansion of the themed hotel-casino resorts.

Potemkin villages plunder the warehouse of building styles and present them anew. Architecture forms a chapter in the great narrative of a new El Dorado, facades are part of the theme-casinos' cinematic method of presentation that is geared towards the perspective of motorists and pedestrians—something Robert Venturi, Denise Scott Brown, and Steven Izenour commented on in their classic book, *Learning from Las Vegas*: "A single shot of the Strip is less spectacular; its enormous spaces must be seen as moving sequences."[2]

Las Vegas is the first completely mediafied city in history, where buildings become signs, facades are information screens that could just as easily be film sets, and the entire metropolis is the crystallization point of a media hype based on glittering surfaces and (disappointed) dreams. Las Vegas owes its rapid rise to its proximity to Hollywood and the mass media, and cleverly increased its fame through films such as *Ocean's Eleven* (1960), *Diamonds Are Forever*, *One from the Heart*, *Bugsy Malone*, *Leaving Las Vegas*, *Casino*,

Mega-hotels like the Excalibur mark the latest stage in the development of Las Vegas; wide walkways and people movers connect them into an almost urban boulevard.

Even Las Vegas Boulevard still has niches and potential for development. Where the themed hotel casino resorts don't reach quite to the street, indeterminate islands multiply.

Showgirls, and the recent remake of *Ocean's Eleven* (2001); cult books such as Hunter M. Thompson's *Fear and Loathing in Las Vegas* with its descriptive subtitle, *A Savage Journey to the Heart of the American Dream*; and innumerable reports in magazines and newspapers. This city leaves nobody cold; in some people it awakens glowing admiration while in others it provokes complete rejection—Michael Herr called it "Helldorado," "Neonatlantis" was Mimi Zeiger's description, and "Zeropolis" Bruce Bégout's. Red or black, all or nothing—there is no in-between in this city of illusions and sleights of hand, where appearances don't last long and seem to change in front of the viewer's eyes. Las Vegas produces material and images as extravagantly as it consumes them; in fact, even the events surrounding its founding could have been taken from a film script full of false trails and Mafia myths. This was where the Rat Pack appeared, where Elvis drank himself to death, and where Britney Spears got married. Las Vegas is sometimes a stage set, sometimes a protagonist, and at other times a catalyst for further chapters in the eternal pursuit of fortune.

Degree of control

Sadly enough, nothing about Las Vegas surprises any more: everybody knows the town before they arrive. The degree of control is amazing. Everything seems perfectly arranged

in this city of illusions that works with focused perspectives and landscapes of staggered backdrops, neon signs, and labyrinthine casino interiors. For a long time now, Las Vegas has ceased to live from the Mob or from games of chance, but rather from its ability to embody a dream world distinct from the run-of-the-mill, puritanical variety. Las Vegas has become a trademark, a label representing perfect entertainment of every kind and a show-piece of the post-industrial service industry. The key to its success is perfect logistics. Tourists are dropped here in much the same way as parts in the production process are delivered to factories—just on time—and during their visit they are moved vertically and

The Eiffel Tower and the Montgolfier balloon at the Paris Las Vegas are reflected like a fata morgana in the Bellagio's water feature.

horizontally from attraction to attraction by monorail, travelator, and elevator. The best way to arrive at such a place is to float in by airplane, where all that remains is to whisk your suitcase from the baggage claim to a waiting taxi or rental car. "Welcome to Fabulous Las Vegas" now blinks where the dreams of yester-year—rundown gaming halls and dilapidated hotels—await new investors. From here the Strip, renamed Las Vegas Boulevard, reaches northwards like an extended runway. To the right and left casino hotels blend to form a collage of "sampled" and "covered" facades, a mega-soundtrack of the pop architecture of the last few decades. Mandalay Bay paints golden stripes across the sky; behind it the 350-foot-high (106 m) Luxor pyramid of dark glass shoots lasers into the air; and New York New York, a gigantic mini-Manhattan, awaits opposite the green cube of the MGM Grand. These are followed by the gamblers' palaces: Paris-Las Vegas, the Bellagio, the Venetian, Caesars Palace, Treasure Island, and the landmark Stratosphere Tower. This 1,149-foot-high (350 m) tower marks the fault line between the classic downtown casinos and the more modern hotel-casino theme resorts on the Strip that epitomize the Disneyfication of Las Vegas.

True Heart of the City

What started as speculative land purchase in the Nevada desert has long since put the old town center around Fremont Street in the shade. Today the Strip forms the true heart of the city while the downtown area is now only a rundown appendage. Whereas initially the speed of the motorized guest dictated the emblematic size of the signs along the road to Los Angeles and of the huge neon advertisements of the casinos—"The big sign and the little building is the rule,"[3] as Robert Venturi and Denise Scott Brown recognized in 1972—the situation now is completely different. The Strip has transformed into a boulevard for strolling guests; the billboards that entice motorists are now to be found only on the parallel highway and, thanks to their presentation, the mega-hotels can even afford to move back somewhat from the Strip and create a seemingly public space—that in fact remains completely private. The "vulgar extravaganza" of the signs and the "modest necessity"[4] of the buildings behind them have recently morphed into a family-friendly stage and show surface, followed by thematically embellished casino hotels. Behind their facades (generally decorated with historical elements) these hotels are in fact a series of high-rise buildings with a splayed, star-shaped plan, arranged one after the other along the Strip. The Mirage, which was the first mega-hotel to open in 1991, launched a new cycle of investment. Treasure Island and the Bellagio followed in 1994 and 1998, respectively. Today

The Empire State Building and the Chrysler Building flank the cityscape of New York New York where the skyline is reduced to its most spectacular buildings. Visitors are best advised to take the roller coaster around the gigantic mini-Manhattan.

eighteen of the twenty largest hotels in the United States are located here. There are over 130,000 rooms for mere mortals, and a number of high-roller suites for the so-called "whales" that gamble up to several hundred thousand dollars in a single day. Whereas for Venturi and Scott Brown the Strip still represented a tripartite harmony of "large open space, big scale, and high speed,"[5] in recent decades not only has the speed of traffic along this former main exit road been reduced, but also the entire feeling has changed dramatically. The Strip has become more urban, at least in regards to the density and the sequence of the casino hotels. Each hotel occupies an entire block and they are connected and networked by bridges and catwalks. Even on the sidewalk there is a lively, southern ease late into the night. Urban qualities have been created by the succession of theme hotels, yet entirely without the services of town planners: the impression is one of a lavishly dimensioned boulevard that you can drive along in comfort or—something increasingly rare in America—can even explore on foot.

Illusionists, Emperors, and Stage Managers

In the open gallery that it calls the Strip, Las Vegas collects images of cities like so many historical landscapes. Bellagio, Monte Carlo, Paris, Venice, and even New York City are lined one after the other to create a *via triumphalis*. But in contrast to the emperors of

antiquity the stagecraft in the media age has no need of real trophies: quotations appropriate to the theme of each hotel casino suffice. A sphinx of sprayed concrete and wood stands guard like a gigantic doorman in front of the Luxor while the Eiffel Tower, reduced by half to 492 feet (150 m), stands like Godzilla astride the Hôtel de Ville. XXL and XS— Las Vegas plays with dimensions and styles. With Paris Las Vegas the architects from Bergman, Walls & Youngblood celebrate their total control of image worlds with leaps in scale and dramatic perspectives, embellishing—or reducing—at will typical Parisian facades, monuments, or urban spaces. Las Vegas architects liquefy scale—Paris is reduced to just a block and Manhattan to a composite incorporating the Empire State and Chrysler Buildings. Urban silhouettes mark the location. Las Vegas does not just borrow images; it cements the perception of the world, our visual repertoire. Entertainment architecture resembles film stills in that it must be instantly recognizable. Complexity is required only if it is ornamental and does not generate any feelings of discomfort. The media city mutates into a chameleon-like meta-metropolis that exploits clichés and develops them even further. Precisely those scenes that flash through your mind when you think of Paris or Venice are arranged in Las Vegas to form a hyper-realistic distillation made up of the true-to-scale Rialto Bridge right beside St. Mark's Square, and the Hôtel de Ville directly under the Eiffel Tower.

Whereas once illuminated signs attempted to entice people from the Strip into the casinos, this role is now played by three-dimensional surfaces that open onto the boulevard like film sets, enriching the optimally detailed landscapes with active elements. The 1,203 water jets of the *Bellagio* water ballet perform to the sound of dramatic music, a few blocks away actors stage pirate battles straight out of Stevenson's *Treasure Island*, or a volcano erupts at regular intervals. Attractions slow down visitors, entice them to stop at determined spots, and increase the likelihood they will enter the casino. Las Vegas is convenient. Why travel half way around the world when in one place you can experience the Chrysler Building as well as the Arc de Triomphe, see a part of the Paris Opéra and

The Campanile and the Rialto Bridge set the tone for the Venetian on Las Vegas Boulevard.

take a snapshot of a singing gondolier? And to top it all off, a romantic candlelight dinner in the Piazza San Marco—in a space that darkens atmospherically to replicate the evening several times during the course of the day—to the strains of a violin beside your table.

It is hardly surprising that the world's most famous illusionists appear in Las Vegas, as the city itself is like a *fata morgana* in the desert. It is often wrongly asserted that architects and designers in Las Vegas create copies—they do not, they instead quote and amalgamate. In this, they resemble fashion designers, or DJs that sample, remix, and cover songs. Ultimately, the constructed illusion surpasses the original, as it eliminates the possibility of annoyances such as the damp moldiness of Venice's side streets, or locals that don't understand English. Here everything functions and everything is controlled: controlled color, controlled music, and controlled emotion. Entertainment architects know the codes of the media society and, under their direction, spaces become surfaces, and facades become consumable signs that can be recalled at any time. Las Vegas demonstrates how easily urban images can be recycled, reconstructed, and activated as backdrops. It is precisely the non-identity of this place somewhere in the desert that makes Las Vegas the ideal location to create this "everywhere, immediately" quality. Ennobled by the use of plasterboard and sprayed concrete, the desert serves as a screen for the leisure and amusement society.

This sophisticated strategy would be unimaginable without the close proximity of the dream factory; Hollywood and Las Vegas live in a symbiotic relationship. While at first the gamblers' city attracted the stars and starlets, and used successful films as inspiration for its casinos, the relationship has long since been reversed. Now Hollywood draws its material from the city of gambling and thus mediafies the setting yet further still. Casinos project and develop Hollywood's image worlds into the future. Every box-office success can become a theme casino, such as Melvin Grossman's Caesars Palace —an homage to the 1962 epic film *Cleopatra* starring Richard Burton as Mark Anthony and Elizabeth Taylor in the title role. And what already exists can easily be changed. Las Vegas is perpetual change, a purposeful and permanent building site: Norman M. Klein speaks in this context of "junking up" the interior as "a useful method of suggesting that the casino is not completely finished [...] the incomplete building stimulates a desire to gamble and perhaps awakens a desire to come back a few months later."[6]

Display of Wonders

The city changes the images in its shop window (the Strip) as you would the displays in a boutique. "Exit closed while we rebuild Rome," reads a posted notice in Caesars Palace, as workers screw on cornices and erect columns. Las Vegas resembles an open warehouse for monumental film sets with competing presentations and layers

The Doge's Palace with a view of Treasure Island, where spectacular shows set new standards in the 1990s in the Disney-fication of Las Vegas.

that at times penetrate each other and at others remain isolated, held together only by the traffic stripes of the street. Over here the elegant world of Monte Carlo, over there escapism and Robinson Crusoe escapades with Aladdin and Treasure Island, and further on Old Europe in the form of the Bellagio, Venetian, and Paris Las Vegas. Those major narratives whose end was celebrated by postmodernism experience a contemporary recycling in the desert of Nevada. Or their definitive end! For this city lives fast: anything that fails to bring profit is rebuilt or torn down. Las Vegas cannibalizes yesterday's dreams. On October 27, 1993, the Dunes vanished in a cloud of dust, followed on November 7, 1995,

Inside the Venetian, the usual times of day no longer apply. The light, artificial sky darkens hourly, creating a romantic evening atmosphere in the bustling St. Mark's Square.

by the Landmark Hotel. Bellagio now occupies the site of the old Dunes, one of the first-generation casinos. Because the miles-long Strip offers good locations and even better sites, it never takes long before gaps are filled. Bellagio and Caesars Palace are expanding; the level of investment is rising. New York New York, with its 2,000 hotel rooms, 4,000 parking spaces, and roller coaster which winds its way around a group of Manhattan skyscrapers shrunk to 30 percent of their original size, swallowed 460 million dollars.

Get them in, Keep them there, and Suck them dry

Pleasure at the press of a button. The architects whom Robert Venturi and Denise Scott Brown accurately described as "urban designers"[7] are only indirectly responsible, although they do supply the backgrounds, rooms, and interiors for the bars and restaurants, shopping malls, showrooms, and gambling halls. The two famous town planners see "lightness, the quality of being an oasis in a perhaps hostile context, heightened symbolism, and the ability to engulf the visitor in a new role" as the link between modern and classic "pleasure zones" such as "Marienbad, the Alhambra, Xanadu and Disneyland."[8] The role played by Las Vegas is a further development of a basic principle of modern theater and art: the spectator forms an intrinsic part of the show and alone determines whether it is a success.

The gondoliers are kept busy in the waterways of the Venetian. La Serenissima, otherwise so confusing, is now readily accessible; its exotic appeal becomes a fleeting backdrop.

But who is this spectator? "A goldmine like Las Vegas breeds its own army,"[9] wrote Hunter S. Thompson, somewhat contemptuously. Today a typical gambler can be described much more precisely, at least in purely statistical terms. He is white, over fifty, and there is a 25 percent likelihood he comes from the neighboring state of California. Apparently there exists the "average man" who spends 3.7 nights and $1,330.02 in Las Vegas: $274.91 for the hotel, $187.32 for food and drink, $94.00 on shopping, $61.01 on transport, $9.16 on sightseeing, $38.39 on shows, and $665.23 on gambling. But the physiognomy of a visitor to Las Vegas can look quite different: for instance a couple that takes advantage of the quickie marriage laws introduced in 1931, stays for around forty-eight hours, and is possibly divorced when they leave the "wedding capital of the world" in a sobered state.

Las Vegas has diversified. The men gamble and the women go shopping; the children whirl in the roller coaster around New York New York—and all these activities take place on different levels that exist independently of each other. Shopping in Las Vegas is itself made up of separate worlds: from the CVS pharmacy chain on the Strip, to a luxury boutique in *Bellagio* and dinner afterwards in *Picasso,* the "best restaurant in Las Vegas". Those surprised by such refinement, and who still have images of cheap buffets and enormous quantities of fast food, probably have not been in the Nevada desert for quite some time. Las Vegas, like its visitors, has reached a state of maturity and is developing into a conference metropolis and "completely normal city."

To understand popular expectations of what comprises a dream world, one must browse the entries by more or less delighted Las Vegas visitors in the semi-official Internet pages and forums. For example D.B. from Texas, who wrote on 20 August 2004 about Aladdin, diagonally opposite Bellagio: "We upgraded for about $30.00 a night to get a view with the fountains. Well worth it. Beautiful!! The buffet was great! If you are there for free drinks they are mainly at the big tables, not the slots …[10]"

What Facades Promise

On the other hand, the gaming casinos still work according to the principle: get them in, keep them there, and suck them dry. Anyone walking along Las Vegas Boulevard today notices, with some amazement, that there are very few cars driving by. It's as if they had been swallowed up by the presentation of the casinos. If there were not, now and then, a few motorists racing their engines between stop lights you would hardly notice the traffic at all. Why should you, after all? Your gaze goes right through it to the other side where it scans, weighs up, and evaluates what the facades there promise. You try to imagine which of these promises could be kept. The street is at best a barrier that prevents tourists from rushing over spontaneously. While the traffic appears to move slower than it actually does, visitors, as they move from one attraction to the next, experience a real deceleration in their pace.

Distance, space, and luxury are the new magic words of the show, and no other casino plays this game with such mastery as the Bellagio when, for instance, the water ballet starts up to the theme from the Pink Panther. The building is concealed, piece-by-piece behind a liquid veil until, in a final orgiastic eruption, compressed-air canons shoot water 250 feet (80 m) into the air, shrouding the entire facade in a curtain of mist. Gradually the casino emerges again.

An inadvertent glimpse behind the scenes of New York New York.

The casinos of Las Vegas: endlessly sprawling, bewildering labyrinths with flashing lights and the at-times-deafening noise of the gaming machines.

The air is still fresh, strips of vapor, as if from an oversized perfume atomizer, float across the lake and along the railing where the crowd of spectators gradually dissolves, some moving slowly along, others entering the casino. The spectacle, the trademark of the luxury casino, has fulfilled its function. Draw their attention, keep them there, and then get them inside along travelators. There is also a different method: no electrically operated doors, no easy entry. To enter the MGM Grand you have to push open doors—twice in fact. Entering the casino is a conscious choice. Heroic Atlas-themed statues greet you, and after a short look from the balustrade to the kidney-shaped show bar you go down the escalator and past the Rainforest Café, where a voluminous rainforest frog with red eyes is intended to interest you in enjoying a cocktail, coffee, or juice under the lianas; you continue past the Grand Buffet, a kind of canteen for gamblers, and then the slot machine hall stands in front of you. These machines apparently provide about 70 percent of the gambling profits, cost around $10,000 each, and have a lifespan of about ten years.[11] The space hums, peeps, and rings like an electronic orchestra warming up. A protective, secret cave that looks like it came straight out of Aladdin's treasure trove opens up before you: dimmed lighting, winding corridors, and abruptly angled spaces whose ends are out of sight. Main aisles in harmonizing colors meander through the gambling zone. Visitors are subtly directed by lighting design and clever transitions in the shape of the space. Casinos are like modern labyrinths that leave gamblers little chance of quickly finding their way around. Las Vegas architecture has mastered the art of transition. Service areas around the

The world of shopping at the Bellagio boasts arcades in the nineteenth-century style, where the most exclusive names are clustered together as though in a modern metropolis.

gaming tables and slot machines permit the gamblers to regain their strength by drinking a coffee or eating a sandwich; they can also dine, take in a show, or shop. And then return to the gaming table. "The madness goes on and on, but nobody seems to notice. The gambling action runs twenty-four hours a day on the main floor, and the circus never ends,"[12]—Hunter S. Thompson's diagnosis a generation ago. Taking a break in the Grand Buffet, Janice smiles enquiringly: "Smoking or non-smoking?" With just this simple question the brunette makes one thing perfectly clear: this is not a café in Manhattan, nor a corner bar in Orlando with a "No Smoking Please" sign at the entrance. No, this is Nevada where smoking is accepted and the only thing prohibited is doing nothing. Even the casual stroller with the greatest endurance will eventually enter somewhere and spend some money. Here there is no longer any difference between Las Vegas and Venice—the labyrinth works: get them in, keep them there, and suck them dry.

Desert, Pilgrimage, Oasis

The oasis in the desert lives thanks to logistics, a constant supply of energy and water. "Sex, air conditioning and traffic planning,"[13] form the basis of urbanity here. Energy is supplied by the Hoover Dam that was built in the 1930s and offers electricity in abundance. The gigantic building site also supplies another resource: workers looking forward

The imposing facades of the Bellagio and Caesars Palace at night dominate the view of the vast reflecting pool.

to the weekend for distraction of any kind, which is just what Las Vegas has to offer. In 1940, the first neon signs blazed above Fremont Street; in 1941, El Rancho opened; and shortly after World War II, the Flamingo. Similar hotel casino complexes based on the same model followed along the Strip, which at the time was still outside the city limits. In 1958, the Stardust casino created an uproar. An illuminated sign transformed a mediocre building into something else: built advertising.[14] What Venturi and Brown, over twenty years later, were to describe as a "decorated shed"—a simple box with an ornamental facade— offered a visual miracle: Kermit Wayne from YESCO (Young Electric Sign Company) magically positioned a metal panel—measuring 238 feet long and 30 feet high (72 x 9 m) and dotted with light bulbs and neon tubes—in the sky above Nevada. The number and size of neon signs exploded in the 1960s: 787 brilliantly illuminated feet (240 m) in front of the Stardust, 138 feet (42 m) high in front of the Sahara, and 197 feet (60 m) high

in front of the Dunes. The Dunes was demolished in 1993 to make room for a new kind of entertainment: the mega-casino theme hotel, which, since the early 1990s, has advanced the concept behind the first theme casino (Melvin Grossman's Caesars Palace from the 1960s) and has completely altered the appearance of the Strip. Las Vegas, created out of nothing, became the center of the entertainment world in a single generation. One generation after that, it liberated itself from the reputation as a Mafia-run gambling town and rose to its position as entertainment metropolis of the world. The Strip-city, the very definition of an artificial leisuretime paradise and model of postmodernism, is so successful that

Corinthian columns, gold, and decorative marble are the hallmarks of the imperial grandeur luxuriously replicated in Caesars Palace.

it already mourns its former reputation as Sin City. The new, family-friendly "Sim City" places its bets on congresses, exclusive boutiques, and shows featuring past-their-prime musicians; and now millions of tourists sit beside the pool and gaze at the 76,000 palm trees and bushes that were planted on the Siegfried and Roy Plaza in 1996.

As "a place of pilgrimage Mecca is the only real competition," Peter Cachola Schmal wrote ironically.[15] Las Vegas and Mecca, the cities in the desert, do in fact have something in common: they both need a great deal of water. Anyone who witnesses the greenness of the lawns along the Strip, and the extravagance of the mystery play in front of the Bellagio, believes that, in Nevada, the desert is alive. Water supplied by the Colorado River is the key to the rapid growth of Las Vegas, but in 1900, the city was nothing more than a watering hole with some grazing land. The railway came in 1905: on May 16, 1905, a special train brought speculators to a real estate auction in a no-mans land and a city was created. Gambling was legalized in 1933, attracting the first soldiers of fortune from Los Angeles, only 270 miles (435 km) away.

Electricity and Criminal Energy

Just how vulnerable this city in the desert actually remains—whose air conditioning systems run at full speed, elevators and ice machines hum, and light bulbs make night into day—is demonstrated in *Ocean's Eleven,* Stephen Soderberg's remake of the 1960 original. In the film, criminal energy succeeds in paralyzing the city: an electromagnetic pulse and the electrical supply fails. Block by block the Strip sinks into darkness, panic prevails, and for a moment Las Vegas seems to be back at the beginning of its meteoric career, a black hole in the Nevada desert. Then the emergency generators spring into life and the eleven casino thieves use the momentary loss of control to carry out their plan, an illusion in the city of illusions. They trick the guards and escape. It is well-made and entertaining cinema—zero risk. The climatic change enters your consciousness rather more dramatically. Traveling across the Hoover Dam today, you see areas of white cliff face left behind by the receding water level of the Colorado River. "The period since 1999 is now officially the driest in 98 years of recorded history," wrote the *New York Times* on May 2, 2004, signaling a substantial drought that makes the twentieth century, with its abundance of water, seem like a major aberration. The western United States is drying up, and even the gambling city where everything seems possible is forced to respond to nature's call. "In Las Vegas the regional water authority is already removing the equivalent of a football field of grass every day from front lawns, playgrounds and golf courses to save on outdoor watering."[16] The Las Vegas of the future will be bigger but in no way greener than the city today. The Garden of Eden might even revert back into a desert.

Architecture on the Fault Line
Between Time and Space

Las Vegas is neon letters that have become a city. Electric noise dominates the architecture as if somebody had forgotten to turn off a gigantic television without reception. Hunter S. Thompson described this flickering as a mix of electricity and drugs that penetrates every crevice. Even the hotel room itself dissolves into a charged aura: "The room was full of powerful electric noise. The TV set, hissing at top volume on a nonexistent channel."[17] The interiors of the casinos attempt to achieve this quality of dematerialization, this detachment of the gamblers from the outside world. In semi-darkness, the eye follows the shimmering colors and carpet patterns, and must constantly refocus. Stimuli rain down on the senses like visual pin pricks.

Although Las Vegas functioned in analog until now, the digital revolution has arrived. Thousands of neon tubes hum and millions of light bulbs warm the entrances, but already architecture and screens blend to form pixel facades. Digital images are wrapped arbitrarily around random facades. Las Vegas has become a stage set crafted under the orders of generations of scriptwriters. The dream couple of recent years are Steve Wynn and Jon Jerde—the creators of the Fremont Experience and Bellagio; they have propagated the Disney-fication of the Strip and the nostalgic reminiscence of Downtown, earning a pretty penny in the process. In 1995, Jerde Partnership erected a glass barrel vault over Fremont Street, the old heart of Downtown Las Vegas, under which the old neon signs of the early days such as "Vegas Vic," the symbol of the Pioneer Casino from Fremont Street, stand like exhibits in a gleaming display case of 2.1 million light bulbs: architecture cast from the same mold, yet at the same time a negation of everything built, as the structures dissolve in cascades of light. Where building is only interior design turned inside out, the real innovations take place behind the scenes, in the technical transmission and refinement of the imagery, the logistics, and the control of visitors. Like every successful business, Las Vegas operates conservatively. This capital of mass culture does not invent trends, but uses them once they begin to appeal to popular taste, inflating them to increasingly new dimensions.

Las Vegas, the real-life movie, created a process that advances as a never-ending remake of itself, but each time with different costumes and new backdrops. It is therefore not surprising that it has absorbed Hollywood's store of images and strategies in its search for stars and starlets, glamour and tragedies, sets and backdrops, myths

Like a moth in the nocturnal desert sky: the facade of the Monte Carlo.

and visions. It is also no surprise that the architecture itself is mediafied, as a medium for narratives and a vehicle for expansive feudal dreams of happiness. According to Norman N. Klein: "Leisure time goals for middle-class families must look feudal. They are based on a close connection between cinema, commerce and tourism that was invented in the 1990s."[18] Public space shrinks, existing only between the gutter and the curb of the boulevard—everything else is private. You are tolerated, as long as you don't misbehave. It is said that 90 percent of Downtown and the Strip are under constant video surveillance.

Las Vegas celebrates total control—not only in the form of the obvious surveillance by means of cameras, security guards, and motion detectors, but also man's control over the whims of nature. Casinos have abolished both time and space. Only the moment counts. Las Vegas functions as the first city to completely embrace the total marketing of popular taste, where consumption needs no context, but rather only an infrastructure of airports and highways connecting it to the world. Las Vegas works as a highly-specialized entertainment machine that identifies popular taste in various images, places, and stories—and then uses them. It doesn't incorporate unique or original elements in its universe; instead, it uses repetition, the platitudes that everyone understands, recognize immediately, and thus, in a way, make one feel at home. Las Vegas has served as the short-term memory of the pop age. Construction and demolition follow each other rapidly. Norman N. Klein estimates the life expectancy of major projects, such as the Luxor that was built in 1993, at around twenty years.[19] The visitors, for their part, respond to the richness of the presentation and switch back and forth between the individual theme casinos, surfing through Las Vegas as they do TV channels. Las Vegas is and has for a long time been part of the global market of images, a cliché of the pre-fabricated dream. In this sense it has left the traditional city far behind. Las Vegas operates visually and acoustically—and no longer with the tools of traditional urban planning.

It is therefore little wonder that there is hardly any public space. Only the traffic infrastructure—airports and streets—has a certain autonomy, everything else is incorporated in the label "Las Vegas." What counts is opulence, an aesthetic that overpowers the eye and the ear. As in a Baroque performance, the two-dimensional replaces the three-dimensional and painted surfaces are substituted for architecture. Where once artificial marble was used, Styrofoam is employed today—a material that gives the impression of being something else. Nobody is surprised by the fact that facades sound hollow, that carpeted floors comfort the feet, and warm colors govern interiors. The profit motive determines the appearance and half-life value of everything that is new.

Size without irony? Presentation without any subtle twist? This is something that can work only in Las Vegas: the capital of illumination, the oasis of illusions. The city determinedly resists the subversion that is a part of the retro cult. Cracks in the illusion occur only by chance when, for instance, mighty facades stand directly opposite vacant lots. Whereas big budget cinema prepares and presents history with detailed precision but in the process often fails to harmonize technology and emotion, Las Vegas seems to possess the formula for creating tangible worlds from fleeting elements; possible only by means of meta-architecture, the mobile stage sets of a city that is completely mediafied. Thanks to Hollywood, everyone has been here once and has seen Downtown, strolled along the Strip, and forgotten themselves in front of the fountains of Bellagio—seen a thousand times and touched just as often. Las Vegas is no longer just a gambling city in the desert and an escape for dreamers, it is a sociological necessity that has developed in the gaps of American society, and that now serves the entire world as a condensed version of all our clichés.

Betty Willis' wonderful farewell to the Gamblers' Paradise.

1 As quoted in Ralph Eue: "Las Vegas im Film: Die Wirklichkeit ist ganz anders" (Las Vegas in film: the reality is completely different), *StadtBauwelt* 143, 1999/36: 2008–2013, p. 2013.
2 Robert Venturi, Denise Scott Brown, and Steven Izenour, *Learning from Las Vegas: The Forgotten Symbolism of Architectural Form*. Revised Edition. (Cambridge MA, 1977), p. 35.
3 Ibid., p. 13.
4 Ibid.
5 Ibid., p. 18.
6 Norman M. Klein, "Scripting Las Vegas: Noir Naifs, Junking Up, and the New Strip," in *The Grit Beneath the Glitter: Tales from the Real Las Vegas*, ed. Mike Davis and Hal Rothman (Berkeley, 2002): 17–29.
7 Venturi, *Learning from Las Vegas*, p. 53.
8 Ibid., p. 53.
9 Hunter S. Thompson, *Fear and Loathing in Las Vegas: A Savage Journey to the Heart of the American Dream* (London, 1993), p. 155. First published in *Rolling Stone* 95 and 96, 1971.
10 travel.travelocity.com/hotel
11 Klein, "Scripting Las Vegas," pp. 17–29.
12 Thompson, *Fear and Loathing in Las Vegas*, p. 46.
13 Eue, "Las Vegas im Film," p. 2009.
14 Alan Hess, Eine kurze Geschichte von Las Vegas (A short history of Las Vegas), *StadtBauwelt* 143, 1999/36: 1980–1987, p. 1982.
15 Peter Cachola Schmal, "Learning from Las Vegas," *deutsche bauzeitung* 11/99, p. 12.
16 Kirk Johnson and Dean E. Murphy, "Drought Settles In, Lake Shrinks and West's Worries Grow," *New York Times*, May 2, 2004, sec. 1, p. 1.
17 Thompson, *Fear and Loathing in Las Vegas*, p. 181.
18 Klein, "Scripting Las Vegas," pp. 17–29.
19 Ibid.

SOUTHDALE MALL
AND
MALL OF AMERICA
A Shopping Universe

Every move is perfect. The cleaning operative pulls out her spray bottle and envelops the plants in a fine mist before removing the dust from the broad leaves. Quick and efficient: the ultimate choreography of cleanliness. And she's gone again. The rippling leaves of the tropical plants nod and gleam as though they came straight from the greenhouse; or fresh off a conveyor belt in a factory producing ancient plastic forests. Altogether, it looks like the cafeteria terrace of a major—let's say—car dealer: white tiles on the floor, bistro chairs, metal railings—extra strong so that no one plunges downwards. This feat is taken care of at the Timberland Twister roller coaster. At the very moment when it's thundering into the valley, a dozen kids scream, and the adults on the terrace take a quick glance before turning back to their soft drinks. They have the best view—on the right, in the corner of the vast hall, the granite mountain, a long water slide called Log Chute, and at the other end of the hall, the seven-story Skyscraper Ferris wheel. If they stand on tiptoes and look down over the railings they can even see the Snoopy Bounce, a huge inflatable Snoopy with a backpack and a blanket, and the Mighty Axe. Welcome to Camp Snoopy, the green heart of Mall of America with around thirty attractions. Welcome to a verdant landscape in the far north, which otherwise is in the grip of winter. Near the twin cities of St. Paul and Minneapolis, broad-leaved plants thrive under a glass roof. Shadows cast by the huge steel beams progress across the floor and the leaves of the 400 trees trucked in from Florida and the Carolinas, drawing one's attention to the system of supports above the visitors' heads.

Until 1982, the Minnesota Vikings played football here and the Minnesota Twins baseball before moving to the Metrodome in downtown Minneapolis. And in 1989, construction work started on the nation's largest retail and entertainment complex, with Camp Snoopy at its green center occupying "seven acres of land beneath 1.2 miles of skylights ... which allows the Park to be lit by 70 percent natural sunlight,"[1] as the website tells us. An astounding place, which—with around forty million visitors—draws

previous double pages:
The name says it all: one of the main entrances to the Mall of America adorned with stars and stripes.

The size of the amusement park at Mall of America is best assessed from above, for instance from one of the restaurant terraces.

larger numbers than Disney World, Grand Canyon, and Graceland put together. A mega-tanker of consumption, a mega-mall that, with a good 520 stores around Camp Snoopy, has become the leading American tourist attraction. The mall is a money machine that produces annual profits of around 900 million dollars and an additional "$1.2 billion outside the project for the state of Minnesota,"[2] as the people from the Jon Jerde Partnership explain. And they should know. After all, they were the ones who drew up the master plan for this dream world in the northern United States. An arsenal of transformations, of logistics, and a carefully balanced mixture of stores; in a word, a miracle where the visitors "spend an average of three hours—three times longer than the national average for shopping malls," to quote the designers. Time spent there is money spent in the same place. A success for Jon Jerde.

Given that the mall is a child of the shopping center, the mega-mall has also invited another relative along, the theme park. In architectural terms, the Mall of America is an astonishing cross-fertilization of factory premises—although having a good time is the only product made at Camp Snoopy—and a harbor grain store, behind whose brick and concrete walls are concealed shops and shopping arcades. Or the Mall could also be a fine looking fortress. It is a mega-mall, but smaller than the largest (for now): the West Edmonton Mall in Alberta, Canada, which was opened in 1985, has a floor area of 5.3 million square feet (nearly 500,000 m^2). However, it seems that West Edmonton is soon to be dethroned by the Mall of Arabia in Dubai. These monster malls offer visitors everything under one roof: shopping, a theme park, and a hotel—if they like. They are the physical manifestation of a widespread longing for a perfectly controlled environment. Alberta and Minnesota both suffer the harshest of winters. While the snow swirls around the houses and the great outdoors is suited only to masochists and reindeer, inside there is warmth and carefree delight.

Victor Gruen, Father of the Mall

If anyone saw the incredible rise of the American mall coming, kept pace with it, encouraged it, and participated in the model, it was the architect and town planner Victor Gruen (as the native of Vienna, Viktor Grünbaum, decided to call himself after he was granted citizenship in 1943). The Father of the Mall arrived to New York in 1938 after the Grünbaums had only narrowly managed to escape the Nazis. Friends of theirs who also attempted to flee were arrested and died in a concentration camp. The Grünbaums

Snoopy enthroned like an
idol above Camp Snoopy,
his own amusement park.

had lost everything, all except their hope of a better world on
the other side of the Atlantic. So, the architect set about making his American Dream come true. At first, the exiles met on a
regular basis and, in June 1939, formed the Refugee Artists
Group, whose activities were supported by, for one, Albert
Einstein. The politically active Viktor Gruen carved out an
astonishing career for himself. Since he had no architectural
qualifications, as yet, he worked together with Morris Ketchum:
"Victor Gruenbaum, designer, Morris Ketchum, architect"—
the pragmatic solution.

At first they were known as shopfitters, creating exclusive
designs in New York. Gruen's designs made an impact and
could even be a little theatrical, as in the case of Lederer's,
a shop selling leather goods opened by the Viennese émigré
Ludwig Lederer on the corner of 5th Avenue and 55th Street.
Gruen transformed the display into an entrance arcade set
back from the busy street, creating a protected area where
shoppers could peruse the items for sale at their leisure. In
Ciro's, next door to Lederer's, Gruen refined the principle and
built an open omega for displaying an assortment of goods,
designed like a fish trap to catch customers. He also created
a temptingly curved facade on 5th Avenue. Inside the shop,
Gruen placed mirrors down the full length of one wall so that
the floor area appeared twice its actual size. The project was
a huge success. "To catch the interest of the window-shy
shopper is the task of the designer,"[3] said Gruen. In 1941,
Architectural Forum published a seven-page profile on the
duo. In May of that year, Gruen divorced and married Elsie
Krummeck, his new partner, before moving to Los Angeles.
The inspired designer imbued the premises of his next client,
the Grayson-Robinson chain, with a sense of optimism, gen-
erosity, and elegance. "This commission would allow Gruen
to take the strategies of the 'sales factory' from Manhattan to
Main Street."[4] But now Gruen and Krummeck were no longer
producing designs from the perspective of the pedestrian,
they were also taking into account the automobile that was
changing America at a shocking rate: distances, perception—
everything. The streamlined Milliron's Department Store,
which opened in March of 1949, showed with what virtuosity
they were able to reflect the new reality of the automobile age
anticipated at the New York World's Fair in 1939. The grand,
vertically articulated temple facade, with its white brim sitting
on the rounded corners like a jaunty summer hat, seemed
to want to tame and absorb the dynamic movement of the
customers rushing by. It unfolded before the shoppers' eyes
and caught their attention with its shadow play, inviting them
to drive up the ramp to the roof—one huge parking lot—to
snatch the best spot, and to descend on the escalators into the
heart of a hall measuring 107,000 square feet (10,000 m^2).

Tropics here, arcades there, but always under the opulent glass roofs that are intrinsic to the mall, like their massive parking lots.

California, which set the trend for the entire United States, soon set about utilizing the available space in a previously unheard-of manner. Gruen enthusiastically greeted the new possibilities this gave to town planners: "The development of Southern California seems so interesting to us because the cities and towns here have mostly been developed since the automobile."[5] The suburbs grew and the city centers—once the business heart of the city—stopped beating. The "autoist" left the pedestrian behind.

Shopping on a Green Meadow

Gruen's next coup was not long in coming. A very different setting but the same problem: explosively expanding suburbs and a dramatic reduction in purchasing power in downtown Detroit. However, the center of the American automotive industry also provided the cure—

Steel, as far as the eye can see. The center of the park: family-friendly attractions under a universal structure with echoes of an industrial construction hall.

a shopping complex on a green meadow that was so attractive that not only locals frequented the Northland Shopping Center (opened in 1954), but also car owners from the surrounding area. Once again, Gruen came up with a stunning concept; and once again, he deployed modernism in the service of an even greater force: consumerism. Like a temple, the four-story Hudson Department Store towers above the surrounding buildings, a cube at the center of the complex, with blocks of stores next to it. The Northland Shopping Center looks like a skillful travesty of Bauhaus architecture with its components orbiting around the central point like satellites. But you have to see the complex from the air in order to gain a realistic impression of its dimensions. It's all about logistics, about how you bring people and materials smoothly together and then separate them again: ramps and approach roads, outer areas, ring roads, and parking lots on different levels. The shopping center sits like a spider in a huge asphalt pentagon of separate parking lots, faintly reminiscent of Chrysler's radial logo and many times larger than the actual shopping complex, whose yards, with plenty of greenery, create something approaching consumption-free public spaces.

Gruen, the town planner, had a vision. He wanted to breathe new life into the suburbs, to re-urbanize them. With a shopping center as the heart of small settlements covering an area of 865 acres (350 hectares), one each in the north, east, west, and south of Detroit, Gruen wanted to redirect and adjust the urban sprawl. The idea was that regional sub-centers would replace isolated, single-purpose districts that were only connected

by gigantic roads and on which human beings were constantly on the move. "Gruen and Smith proposed the shopping center as suburbanites' salvation from ... social isolation,"[6] writes Jeffrey Hardwick, and it was precisely this missionary zeal, the desire to help to create a better world, that led Gruen to make one major error. Like the centrifugal satellites of the Northland Shopping Center, which attracted up to 60,000 visitors on weekdays and up to 100,000 on weekends, this shoppers' paradise—only accessible by automobile—simply accelerated the process of urban sprawl, as though Gruen had discovered the catalyst for an irreversible reaction. His model for a shopping center was successful; unbelievably successful as it met the wishes of a whole generation that, in the postwar boom years at the latest, had become a generation of consumers who demanded choice and good value, and in the same place. Gruen personally designed 43 million square feet (4 million m²) of shopping space, and the Northland Shopping Center became the epitome of a new culture, in part—or perhaps specifically—because his ambitious plans for a new urbanism never came to fruition. The model set the standard for a new type of building, and was copied throughout the United States. "Mercantilism is the deepest root of that specific cultural form of urbanism," commented Otto Kapfinger in his discussion of Gruen's rise as the "pioneer of the shopping center."[7]

The first mall in the world: Southdale Center, now refurbished in the spirit of postmodernism.

All Under One Roof

It was now only one short step to the Mall, that weatherproof, fully-covered, air-conditioned shopping environment. And Gruen was ready to take that step, even if he jokingly referred to the mall as a modern version of the Milan Galleria, which it could never become; after

The "Golden Trees"—two large bronzes by Harry Beroia—look almost like aliens in this postmodern scenario.

all, air conditioning is wholly alien to the towering, vaulted Italian arcades that soared unproductively into the sky. The use of air conditioning meant optimizing the internal flow of traffic, connecting any open areas to shops, and eradicating passages without a function. In the case of the Southdale Center in Minneapolis, opened in 1956, Gruen worked on three levels. On the lowest level, in the basement so to speak, were the services, children's play areas, and offices; above that were two more levels linked by a three-story roofed garden atrium. Much of what had been promised at the Northland Shopping Center was taken up and perfected in the Southdale Center: arcades and open areas all under one roof. Instead of having just one anchor store and according it temple-like splendor, Southdale Center relies on polyvalence. Two large stores form two poles, with around seventy smaller stores stretching between them, so that the mall seems a little like a set of dumbbells, slightly rotated and dynamically distorted. In the middle is the atrium with galleries, plants, and light on all sides. In a second circle, there is parking for 5,600 vehicles, divided into fifteen sectors distinguished by different animals, from the giraffe to the rooster. The national press was effusive in its praise. *Life* magazine acclaimed Southdale as the "splashiest Center in the U.S.," as an incredible combination of "goldfish pond, birds, art, and 10 acres of stores all ... under one Minnesota roof."[8] Photographs of the opening on October 8, 1956, show Gruen in an inimitable pose, his back to the balustrade, explaining the wonders of the mall to the visitors. As his left hand makes a sweeping gesture, his right hand, holding a cigarette, signals with the thumb towards one of the atriums.

The Golden Trees—two large bronzes by Harry Beroia—are still standing. They recall the elegance of way back then, when luxury still had a clear form and was contained within a fluid, unobtrusive space-continuum. Nowadays Southdale is only a shadow of its former self. Lumpy postmodern columns and candy colors obscure the clear shapes of the 1950s; later additions and an extra fifty shops crowd the mall. In 1988, the center underwent a general refurbishment; an annex was added to Dayton's Department Store and the interior was largely redesigned with rows of bronze-colored uplighters and balustrades. The bronze trees look like strangers, standing there under a roof that was once their own. Only the huge skylight in the shape of the saddleback roof still seems to be original.

Gruen had struck gold, and Southdale set the standard: 1,800 regional shopping malls were built along the same lines as Southdale, as its official brochure still mentions. Within ten years, Victor Gruen Associates became one of the twenty largest architectural practices in the United States. Gruen explained the credo that underpinned the partnership founded in 1950 by himself, Rudolf Baumfeld, and three other associates: "We do not belong to the Form Givers. We have no desire to create new fashions in architecture. There is little value in the building of buildings alone. The only thing that really matters is taking a whole area and creating an environment, comfortable and convenient for the people who live there, work there, or shop there. It is environmental architecture that really calls for imagination today. Architectural style is secondary."[9] Architecture as a

Little is left of Victor Gruen's Southdale Center, yet the later additions haven't completely spoiled the architect's elegant design.

tool and component in shaping the environment—Gruen headed a movement that soon had no need of the Master. And yet, the suburbs failed to become more compact with the arrival of the malls as Gruen hoped; in fact, the opposite occurred. What's more, not all visitors were so impressed by the opportunity to do their shopping in a glass box. When Frank Lloyd Wright visited Southdale shortly after it was opened, he dismissed the design with a few sentences which no critic could have formulated more devastatingly: "In all this there should be increased freedom and graciousness. It is wholly lacking," was his comment to Gruen in the visitors' book. In Wright's opinion, the idea was ill-advised: "You have tried to bring downtown out here. You should have left downtown downtown."[10] Gruen responded to his critics, penned numerous texts, and in 1964 published the book *The Heart of Our Cities: The Urban Crisis, Diagnosis and Cure*. Amongst other things, he proposed the pedestrianization of downtown areas, an idea first explored in the Netherlands in 1952. Even if his own spectacular plans for the rejuvenation of the center of Fort Worth fell foul of the local authorities who only paid lip service to his proposals, at least one journalist recognized the stature of Gruen's plans for breathing new life into the dead body of the city: "It's the first city dream plan in the United States," declared the *Fort Worth Press*.[11]

Southdale was officially opened on October 8, 1956, and soon became a magnet for everyone. Ultimately even the annual ball of the Minneapolis Symphony Orchestra took place in this shopping paradise, which was also the largest roofed space in the area. Twenty-six years later Southdale replaced Downtown Minneapolis as the region's premier shopping destination. Logically, there was only one way of improving on Southdale: the mega-mall. America's largest shopping paradise lies only around twenty minutes by car from the first mall. On June 14, 1989, the moment had come: groundbreaking for the Mall of America. Its praises are sung from the moment one lands at the airport, and hotels vie with each to be the closest accommodation to the Mall. Bloomington alone boasts thirty-three hotels within minutes of the Mall of America.

"So fun ..."—Mega-Sales and More

Mall of America, the largest shopping paradise in the United States, which opened on August 11, 1992, near the twin cities of Minneapolis and St. Paul, entices shoppers from the four corners of the globe. Bus- and planeloads of people converge on the Mall of America, transformed into a holiday destination that provides a handsome return on the 650 million dollars invested in it. In 520 stores, 22 restaurants, and 27 fast-food outlets spread over three floors, typical American merchandise is for sale; and at reasonable prices as Minnesota doesn't charge sales tax on food and clothing. "Shop till you drop" is the motto, and while the parents do just that, the kids can have their fun on the roller coaster and the other giant toys at Camp Snoopy, which is—with a floor space of 1.6 million square feet (150,000 m^2)—the largest enclosed amusement park in the United States. Hundreds of millions of shoppers have spent their money there: "Do the

monster mall: It's more than stores," promises Joseph Gyure of the *Waco Tribune Herald*,[12] and he's right. A mega-mall is like a huge machine that connects people and materials at top speed, provides a setting where the hoped-for transaction takes place, and separates them again. In addition to this, it is also a three-dimensional textbook on applied sociology: what finds favor stays and grows; what no longer fits, disappears. Malls reflect the society in which they flourish; they are perfectly balanced and choreographed, with anchor stores at the corners that draw the visitors from one end to the other. Mall of America of course has four anchor stores, placed one at each corner like oversized pillars, like fortifications: Nordstrom, Sears, Bloomingdale's, and Macy's. Not surprisingly, they are the major department store players. In between them, the game of the designers and sociologists plays out in precisely calculated rest areas, recuperation spots, and gastronomy, providing perfectly timed nourishment for the battle for the best offers. One word about the offers: many of the visitors are aware that the prices are higher here, but are more than willing to put up with this because they are, after all, shopping at a top tourist destination. The hunt for bargains is replaced by the ambience of the shopping experience. And that, too, is no mean feat on the part of the team working with Jon Jerde, who designed the largest retail complex as a series of four distinct shopping areas: North Garden, East Broadway, South Avenue, and West Market. Indeed the designers went even further: "To make the enormous Mall of America easy to navigate, Jerde modeled it after a small city."[13] A whole city for consumers; a new city after downtown Minneapolis had lost the race with the much smaller Southdale Center as early as 1982. A dream town, which has nothing of the usual urban problems and limitations, contradictions and faults, but also a town entirely unsuited for making last-minute smaller purchases, to judge by the comments of some who live nearby: "It is always crowded and overpriced for the same thing you can get from any other mall within 10 miles for much less,"[14] says loki13; and BeanoCook adds: "I live near by yet I only go there with guests from out of town."[15] Mall of America is a new category—a separate world—using modern montage techniques to present more concentrated shopping sensations and experiences that could not be further from small town life. Veritably, an urban entertainment center!

The Mall of America is memorable for one thing above all—its size.

The overall design of Mall of America resembles a huge canyon spanned by bridges on three levels. Above the people's heads is a vast glass roof, an echo of Paris or Milan. But the resemblance ends there, for it is huge, but it is rarely hugely impressive, like Canal City Hakata on Fukuoka, also designed by Jon Jerde and opened in 1996. Presented as a shopping experience, the Japanese mall takes the picture of the canyon literally and includes water and rock formations copied from nature, which are infused—or should one say obscured—by the idea of an urban shopping arcade. Mall of America looks rather brutal in comparison, focused solely on overwhelming visitors by its sheer size: "Walking distance around one level—.57 miles,"[16] declares the website's facts page, and the stores laid end-to-end would cover a distance of 4.3 miles (6.9 km). Shopping as jogging. Master mall-builder Alfred Taubman has come to certain conclusions as to the optimal size. In his view, three city blocks is the best length because visitors generally don't want to walk any further than that, and a third floor is problematic as visitors tend to walk in one direction on one floor and back along the other.[17] Nevertheless, Mall of America easily copes with its three stories and packs the elliptical shopping levels with restaurants and food courts. The atmosphere also changes floor by floor, becoming brighter, more glittery, and reminiscent of the promenade deck of Star Trek's Deep Space Nine. The sheer size of what is after all the "largest indoor family theme park in the country"[18] expands the usual limits of logistics, and the next extension is already in the cards. Phase II is the name of the project designed to propel the giant into a new orbit. IKEA has already signed on; hotels, a business center with conference facilities and recreational, fitness, and spa facilities are to follow. A whole town is springing up around Fortress Mall of America, which may present a rough exterior but which is as soft at heart as the soft ice cream at Camp Snoopy. Up to "5.7 million square feet of new development ... on 42 acres of adjacent property."[19]

Mega-Malls and Success

In Germany at present there are 481 shopping centers with a trading area of upwards of 86,000 square feet (8,000 m^2), and in the last four years, the total trading area has increased by almost 25 percent.[20] While impressive by European standards, it is nothing in comparison to the United States: in 2003, the malls in the US had a turnover of 240 billion dollars;[21] in 2002, consumer spending in malls accounted for around 70 percent of the gross national product, equaling an amount greater than what most other industrialized nations spend. No wonder mega-malls are regarded as a model of mega-success, which in itself goes unquestioned. Those who do dare to criticize this success are easily dismissed as merely jealous when they bemoan the malls' disproportionate size, their botched architecture, and a society that has run off the rails. Size is certainly an element that the malls know how to exploit, that they have to exploit. Bigger is better, and the concept is justified by its success. The one-time role of cathedrals—structures with a presence and an atmosphere that send shivers down the spine of the faithful—is now

filled by these temples of consumerism. The occupancy rate of retail space at Mall of America is an incredible 99 percent. Wander along the different thoroughfares and you won't see a single store front that is darkened, curtained off, or even shabby; and vacancies that might occur are skillfully disguised, for nothing kills sales as effectively as the whiff of bankruptcy. You can see it happening in other areas. One store closes and the store next door doesn't hold on for much longer; the neighbor thinks about going elsewhere and the retail reputation of the whole street is ruined. In the Mall, the management steps in. It sorts out the different outlets, checks the mixture, and constantly adjusts it to fit changing needs. The Mall is a living creature: 11,000 employees work here year round; on public holidays and in the summer, the numbers increase by 15 percent to around 13,000. Parking for almost as many vehicles—12,550—is provided in two strategically placed multi-level car parks, which rise like monoliths at the eastern and western ends of the complex.

It is impossible not to be affected by the Mall of America. It is a manifesto: shopping as a way of life, consumption as a pleasure principle in a mega-center of distraction. The shift in the usual perspectives catches one off-guard, until the picture suddenly tips right over. The mall is now the city, and the city, well, the city is history, as NoTaFaN will tell you: "If you're in the mood for a major urban shopping center, the MoA is the place to go. Everything imaginable can be found there, and it's fun just to go and see."[22] There is even a wedding chapel, although some might be a little uneasy at the thought of tying the knot in this temple of consumerism. So fun!

A cathedral to consumption: different sections of the Mall of America have distinctive styles, to keep the visitors' senses alert.

1 info.campsnoopy.com/Fun/Facts.htm
2 www.jerde.com. As usual, the figures vary considerably, depending on the source. The figures used here give an idea of the sheer size of the project.
3 M. Jeffrey Hardwick, *Mall Maker: Victor Gruen, Architect of an American Dream. Philadelphia* (Philadelphia, 2004), p. 29.
4 Ibid., p. 49.
5 Ibid., p. 95.
6 Ibid., p. 120.
7 Otto Kapfinger, "Victor Gruen und Rudi Baumfeld: Traumkarriere einer Partnerschaft," in Matthias Boeckl, ed., *Visionäre & Vertriebene: Österreichische Spuren in der modernen amerikanischen Architektur* (Berlin, 1995):255–79, p. 255.
8 Hardwick, *Mall Maker: Victor Gruen*, p. 145.
9 Walter Guzzardi, "An Architect of Environments," *Fortune*, January 1962, p. 77. As quoted in Hardwick, *Mall Maker: Victor Gruen*, p. 29.
10 "Minneapolis crucified by Architect," *Rapid City Journal*, November 29, 1956. As quoted in Hardwick, *Mall Maker: Victor Gruen*, p. 151.
11 As quoted in Hardwick, *Mall Maker: Victor Gruen*, p. 173.
12 Joseph Gyure, "Do the Monster Mall: It's More than Stores," *Waco Tribune-Herald*, January 23, 2005.
13 www.jerde.com
14 www.rateitall.com/i-9666-mall-of-america.aspx
15 Ibid.
16 www.mallofamerica.com/about_moa_facts.aspx
17 *Süddeutsche Zeitung*, October 22, 2004, no. 246, p. 17.
18 www.mallofamerica.com/about_moa_facts.aspx.
19 Ibid.
20 *Süddeutsche Zeitung*, November 26, 2004, no. 275, p. V2/1.
21 Wolfgang Kunath, "Joggen auf bewachtem Parkplatz," *Frankfurter Rundschau*, August 7, 2004.
22 www.rateitall.com/i-9666-mall-of-america.aspx

TROPICAL ISLANDS
AND
THE PALM
Last Resorts

The Beach—not a word, but a state of mind, an attitude about life originally known only to surfers, but introduced into our living rooms during prime time by the *Bay Watch* team. Nowadays anyone can try it out for a couple of weeks on Mallorca, Bali, or at Daytona Beach —wherever. Is there anything that stirs the dreams and desires of our adventure-hungry society so deeply as that formula of sunsets, sand, and sea, which is mercilessly exploited the world over—white sand, palms, waves lapping onto a crescent beach? Open any travel brochure and there they are: exotic destinations for dream holidays, all-inclusive, right down to the drink in the holidaymaker's hand. Temporary escapism—a Robinsonade for the stressed workers from Western society. What was once for the privileged few is now a perfectly natural part of the annual round of events. It is a chance to switch off from the office, to let body and soul off the hook. The locations become ever more exotic, and the demand ever greater. In the search for authenticity, the most distant regions are opened up and developed. First globetrotting, then study trips, then package holidays—a sort of anti-gentrification of the rest of the world. No wonder new oases are being created today from sun, sand,

previous double pages:
The Palm and The World off Dubai's coast

Replicating reality, or rather, surpassing reality: the Japanese Ocean Dome— according to the "Guinness Book of Records," the biggest, roofed waterworld anywhere on Earth.

The blue lagoon is already in place; now the plants just have to grow.

and water, artificial worlds that combine comfort and guaranteed sun. The Ocean Dome, erected in 1999 in Miyazaki, Japan, directly next to one of the largest conference centers in the country, has a roof that simply closes when the weather turns foul, and the holiday-makers—in fact located only a few hundred yards from the Pacific Ocean—can enjoy the perfect scenery and the steady swell of the waves at a constant temperature of 86 degrees Fahrenheit (30 °C). We now have beach holidays forever—at any time, whatever the season.

The demand for artificial paradises is increasing. Human beings are creating their own environments, their dream worlds, everywhere and on a grand scale. Tropical Islands in the sand of the Marks outside Berlin—the biggest cantilevered structure in the world—is protected from the vicissitudes of the weather in the northern hemisphere, sheltered in an eternal spring. And for those in the mood for an island, there is Dubai's mega-project, The Palm and its offspring.

A Gleaming Bubble in the Middle of Nowhere

That is what it looks like when the energy that goes into work is transferred from produc-tion to reproduction, creating an icon of the new leisure and adventure society: a gleaming bubble in the middle of nowhere. Thirty miles (50 km) southeast of Berlin is where the tropics start, contained in a 251-foot-high (107 m) shell of steel and plate glass. What

was once a plan to construct heavy-load airships—giant zeppelins that could transport materials though the air to construction sites—amongst the pine trees and shrubs of the Mark Brandenburg, is now a cylindrical hall—1,181 feet long and 689 feet wide (360 x 210 m)—where dreams are being manufactured; leisure dreams of gentle summer evenings á la *dolce vita* on fine Italian sand in shady niches under the 500 species of tropical trees imported from Southeast Asia. With the initial 300 million dollars poured into the ambitious CargoLifter project, the largest cantilevered hall in the world was built; when the speculative bubble burst, an alternative use had to be found, and this turned out to be an amusement park on a previously unknown scale. The Malaysian entrepreneur Colin Au spent 14.9 million dollars (12.7 million euros) to become the owner of this hall, large enough to hold half of Potsdamer Platz and the whole of the Statue of Liberty. In it he set about constructing an oasis with a Bali lagoon, a tropical village, a rain forest, a palm-lined south-sea beach, and a show stage: features that were designed and optimized by experts from all over the world. The tropical trees were freshly planted on the 46-foot-high (14 m) artificial hills in the center of the hall. Beneath them are 2,200 changing booths, the kitchens, and the central services for the site.

A Million Square Feet of Steel and Glass

No church nave, no opera house, no concert arena can prepare visitors for what they will find under the 1.2 million square feet (110,000 m^2) of steel arches and glass. One's sense of scale becomes confused. Men working on the facade, rappelling down the gleaming silvery skin and the solar sails to fit the 10.2-foot-thick (3.1 m) ETFE foil isolation units, look no bigger than flies. You would have to be a Tarzan to fully grasp the dimensions of the hall, swinging from support to support 351 feet (107 m) above the ground in order to properly take in the three-part adventure world; from the crescent-

The biggest cantilevered hall in the world is located on a former Soviet airfield near Berlin.

shaped south-sea bay, with its terraced levels for the jungle excursion, to the liver-shaped Bali lagoon on the other side. Built in 2001 by the Munich firm SIAT, the hall now boasts Europe's largest stage, 459 feet long by 164 feet wide (140 x 50 m), with canoes, galleons, and special effects. Images are projected onto a water curtain, providing sunrises and sunsets for enthusiasts who spend the night in tents before stepping back into the tropical ocean. Five million liters of water—at a bathtub temperature of 82 degrees (28 °C)—gently lap against the edges of a steel tub; in the Bali lagoon the rippling water is even kept at a temperature of 88 degrees (31 °C). Environmentalists complained that to set the temperature of 6.8 million cubic yards (5.2 million m^2) of air at a steady 82 degrees (28 °C) would require as much energy as a small town, but when it is fully booked with approximately three million visitors annually, Tropical Islands in fact uses less energy than a regular indoor swimming pool, around six kilowatt hours per guest. One and a-quarter miles (2 km) of insulation materials were used for the door hinges alone, 16-inch-thick (40 cm) foil tubes to keep out the cold of the Mark Brandenburg. No one knows just how much jet fuel would be saved if millions of people were to spend the holidays in the Brandenburg tropics. A staff of 375—which is to double with the building of two new hotels—takes care of the sun-hungry masses. Tropical Islands promises a man-made paradise with 82 tons of screws and 140 tons of paint. Colin Au knows all about projects on this scale having already been involved, as an investor, in the construction of the biggest amusement complex in the world: Foxwoods Resort and Casino in Connecticut. The concept of Tropical Islands seems to be diametrically opposed to his successful project in Malaysia: more than sixteen million guests visit the Genting Highland Resort at an altitude of 6,560 feet (2,000 m) with refreshing temperatures ranging between 68 and 77 degrees Fahrenheit (20–25 °C). When it is 91.5 degrees (33 °C) in the shade, this sounds like a nice alternative.

On the 1,235-acre (500-hectare) site of a former Russian air force base, with hangars extending across the landscape like so many oversized molehills—Tropical Islands. It is

It's impossible even to start taking in the dimensions of the onetime airship construction hall.

still possible to make out the numbers of the different runways: the 0.6-mile-long (1 km) tracks where cars are now parked, super-hard concrete reinforced with steel the thickness of a man's thumb. The detritus of the Cold War: crumbling walls, miserable huts, and dusty roadways, and at the center of it all, the airship construction hall, once a symbol of technological advancement covering an area equal to eight football fields, and now a luxury tropical resort. In Brandenburg, instead of contending with sticky evenings under a mosquito net and daily downpours at noon, visitors find fine Italian sand on the beach, trees from Thailand, and folklore from Bali to Rio. Tropical Islands is a three-dimensional travel brochure; according to its own publicity, the hall is equivalent to the "largest cruise ship sailing for the tropics." At the very least, it marks a first leap into the global leisure industry, which clones locations and relocates landscapes: Venice at the Venetian in Las Vegas, Rottenburg-Nürnberg as part of the German Village at Disney World in Orlando, palms in the Mark Brandenburg and, before we know it, skiing in Dubai. The greater the contrast between inside and outside, between the perceived and actual surroundings, the more appealing the attraction. While the car is freezing up outside, guests bask on the heated tropical beach, sipping cocktails at 82 degrees in the shade, and party on the beach until the break of dawn. In the midst of it all, the artificial hill and a grove of tropical plants. Between the saplings a paths winds its way through the landscape, which looks from the air like a loose labyrinth, a minimal interruption in this eternally uplifting, eternally warm paradise by a tropical beach.

Soon tourists will be basking on an artificial beach.

Paradise is an Island in the Sun

In the archive of the Institute for Paradise Research,[1] you will find the following: "My paradise is a small island with a white sandy beach and a Turkish sea that the sun shines down all day long. I have a beautiful, big, white house that I designed myself on a hill in the middle of the island, so that every day I look at the sea from every window and watch the sun going down,"—one woman's response when questioned about her personal picture of paradise. "On my island there's a tennis court, a huge swimming pool, a fitness suite, and all sorts of other sports equipment etc. And there's a boat to go and visit my friends with. I can invite whoever I want to my island; my boyfriend is the only one who is always on the island with me." It is a mixture of the Aegean Sea, the *Blue Lagoon*, and

The contours of the islands Palm Jumeirah, Palm Jebel Ali, and Palm Deira are visible with the naked eye even from outer space.

Club Med. The owner of this Isle of the Blessed sees herself as a well-toned, eternally young woman who could easily take part in a TV ad or go in for a triathlon, if she felt like it. Although she expressly denies recourse to religious, moral, or ideological concepts, her Arcadian paradise draws on both classical imagery and the fitness cult of recent years. There are no private utopias any more, no ideas that are not shaped by convention, especially in a society that celebrates the freedom of the individual. Places and people come together, immaculate physiques and a glowing setting are inextricably intertwined; the occupants of this paradise are young, healthy, attractive, sun-soaked, beautiful, bright, and their house, white. "We're around 21, a man and a woman, my boyfriend's got perfect skin (me too, of course), we're both slim and taut and toned, and can eat whatever we want without putting on weight!!! And, of course, we're still sweet and fun."[2]—a slightly doubtful afterthought like a plea for forgiveness. Evidently, the anonymous participant in the survey felt a little uneasy at the thought of her perfect world and physical prowess. The completely new beginning turns out to be no more than an old cliché: ever since the days of Robinson Crusoe, the sun, the sea, and an island have been permanent features of other worlds, be they paradise or just a holiday destination.

The Ultimate Dream World

It's astonishing how well this dream picture fits the ultimate dream world of The Palm: an island universe in the Persian Gulf; a second Atlantis created from dozens of artificial islands as the ultimate holiday destination for jet-setting tourists who, searching for new locations, take a trip to the United Arab Emirates where the swimming pools are cooled in the summer like the drinks at the bar. And the website paints a similar fairytale, its blunt sales pitch focusing on one thing above all—money. "Once again Dubai is going to create a new wonder of the world. After Burj Al Arab, the only 7* hotel of the world, now The Palm is under progress. The Palm consists of 2 artificial islands: The Palm Jumeirah and The Palm Jebel Ali. Both islands are heaped up in a palm form. The inner part of the island consists of 17 whisks and receives through it a diameter of 5 kilometers. Each of the two islands is offering 50

luxury hotels, 2500 exclusive beach villas, 2400 apartments with sea look, marinas, recreational parks, restaurants, shopping centers and much more. About 2000 villas were already sold from Palm Jumeirah within the first 3 weeks. Many of it already become available on the second market with a profit of approx. 30%."[3] A third island, Palm Deira, is already in the planning stages. Obviously a profitable investment. An oasis of the rich and powerful: a gated community for all those who can pay the entrance fee? It's not without reason that the investment site talks up the exclusivity and secluded nature of the islands: "The estates and its visitors only have admission to this exclusive community, otherwise, the families enjoy their life in a uniquely secure environment."[4] While the islands of The Palm are connected to the mainland by bridges, The World has an even more exclusive clientele in its sights, with 300 islands that can only be reached by boat or by helicopter.[5] A preview of a brave new globalized world in which Dubai can compete with classically luxurious locations like Monte Carlo. We live in a world of achievement that puts places on the map, and systematically develops them with an eye to the *Guinness Book of Records*: the biggest mall, the most luxurious luxury hotel, the most expensive private beach. Dubai is breaking new ground, quite literally: it is creating attractions for a time when the country's oil revenues will be a thing of the past, and other sources of income have to be found. A clever investment or just money buried in the sand? Dubai is all about strategic investment in the global competition to be the best. In Abu Dhabi, dream worlds are created, such as the Emirates Palace, with a gateway

Glowing like a dream in "1001 Nights": the Emirates Palace in Abu Dhabi — a palatial hotel on a truly imperial scale.

following double pages: Night view of the Emirates Palace

In the Emirates Palace, things are not what they appear to be. It may look like a digital image but it is completely real — a dream of concrete and ornament with gleaming mother-of-pearl surfaces.

that is reminiscent of the Arc de Triomphe in Paris and an atrium that puts St. Peter's in the shade.[6] With 394 rooms and suites—a pearl on the chain of Kempinski hotels—it is reputed to have cost 1.7 billion dollars to build. Reports from the first travelers to make it there sound like tales from *1001 Nights*, their astonishment spring-loaded with figures, exact details, and precise examples such as the descriptions of the 20 fountains with the 8,000 plants that transform the garden into an oasis, a paradise on Earth, where above all no visitor is supposed to feel "at home." Gold leaf and marble, dazzling splendor, a place that is clearly not of this world: or perhaps just showy luxury?

1 www.ipfo.de
2 Ibid.
3 http://www.dubai-invest.net/catalog/ the_palm_jumeirah.php
4 Ibid.
5 http://www.stern.de/lifestyle/reise/ fernreisen/index.html?id=533080
6 Tomas Niederberghaus, "Es ist alles Gold, was glänzt," *Die Zeit*, 7/2005, February 10, 2005, pp. 65–66.

DREAM WORLDS RELOADED

Theme-Park Cities and Game Worlds

The twentieth century succumbed to three dreams: the intoxicating rationalism of the Plan Voisin and the new capital city of Brasilia, the allure of the media-made world in Las Vegas, and the longing for the slowness of Celebration. While the rational, rigorously organized city of modernity has come up against its own limitations, and New Urbanism seeks to escape the world in its own untimely way, the march of the media continues apace. At the beginning of the new millennium, the ideal city has lost its original appeal. Its legacy has been left to commercial dream worlds, mixtures of the most advanced architecture, marketing, and entertainment: paradises of consumption, oases of precisely circumscribed pleasure, which even capitalize on excesses and extremes of the kind found in Las Vegas in a manner acceptable to their own target groups. Yet, this phenomenon is now no longer the preserve of theme parks, mega-malls, and airports. Under the influence of theming, possibly the most successful architectural strategy in recent decades, perfectly ordinary towns and medium-sized cities are changing. They are becoming consumable and—however paradoxical it may sound—interchangeable, as people chase after something special: the unique attraction. Who knows of Metzingen, Wertheim, or Wolfsburg? Metzingen and Wertheim have turned into FOCs (Factory Outlet Centers), which also happen to be towns. Wolfsburg is becoming an automotive theme park. Evidently, the fear of having a bad image is not as great as that of having no image at all.

Urban Amusement Centers

There are many places nowadays where it's clear that reality and simulation have changed places. For instance Wolfsburg, which became the motor of the postwar economic miracle in Germany symbolized by the Volkswagen Beetle produced there, is now attempting to negotiate the leap from manufacturing to the service sector. Volkswagen is transforming Wolfsburg into an *Autostadt*—a car city. Directly next to its own factory premises, the company has created—at a cost of 505 million dollars (430 million euros)—a theme park where the car reigns supreme. The new *Autostadt* is all about the total marketing of a single product. Science and art centers form part of the package, as do the Cinemaxx theater, water parks, and a five-star hotel, which is of course particularly glad to welcome Volkswagen managers and guests of the company. Ever since its early days in the 1930s, this town, positioned strategically on the Mittellandkanal and on the main rail connection between the Ruhr Area and Berlin, has had only one *raison d'être*: mobility. The autobahn was to mark the beginning of the mobilization of society under a national-socialist regime. Customers were to reach the town by train and to collect their new cars themselves in the factory. On July 1, 1938, the Nazis founded the "Stadt des KdF-Wagens"[1] on an undeveloped site; and on May 25, 1945, the Allies renamed the town Wolfsburg. By the end of the war almost 70 percent of the Volkswagen factory had been

The town of Wertheim, Germany, has turned into a factory outlet.

destroyed, but by 1951 it was already producing 105,000 cars annually, which rose to 800,000 in the 1960s. In ten years, Wolfsburg doubled its population; by 1960, it stood at 65,000, with 60 percent of the working population employed at Volkswagen. Wolfsburg became the fourth richest city in the Federal Republic of Germany. The oil crisis of 1974, however, led to a reduction of the work force at Volkswagen of 10,000 over two years.

It was essential that the town should actively market itself in order to escape the fluctuations in the car industry on which Wolfsburg was 100 percent dependent. The idea was that the town itself should become an *Erlebnisstadt*— a city offering visitors a very special experience. While the German pavilion at Expo 2000 in Hanover exuded the charm of a medium-sized car dealer, not far away in Wolfsburg Volkswagen was creating a whole world devoted to the car. The new *Autostadt* transposed the fascination with mobility into a choreography of buildings and design studios. Arctic white, silver, and pitch black: the individual pavilions of the daughters

Audi, Bentley, Lamborghini, Seat, and Škoda are at the heart of a 62-acre (25 hectares) fjord landscape by the Mittellandkanal. Prospective buyers and new owners collecting their cars can meander through the pavilions and perhaps be inspired to add this or that extra to their purchases. In all cases, however, all visitors should find their way to the Customer Center, a glass ellipsoid with a gigantic pylon, where the dream car is handed over. It has something about it of an airport when the make and model appears on all the displays, along with the name of its future owner. While the customer takes a seat in the Water Bar, and sips at a glass of strawberry soda, the car is already awaiting collection in one of two glass cylinders. Every forty seconds a brand new vehicle comes off the production line, rises up twenty stories in a series of elevators, and disappears off towards the Customer Center. The heart of *Autostadt*, visible from afar, beats to its own two-cylinder rhythm. The extension is designed to raise and lower up to 2,000 vehicles per day in a total of six glass towers, a phalanx of progress that over-

Taking the elevator to car heaven:
cars ready for collection are parked
in huge glass cylinders.

shadows—and distracts attention from—the
factory premises behind them. Although the old
power plant with its brickwork still sets the tone
in terms of architecture and reminds us of the
machine aesthetics—steel, sweat, and soot—
of the last century, *Autostadt* is far ahead
of this. It celebrates not only the product, but
also presents it as part of an all-embracing
lifestyle. The information age runs rings around
the production process. Industry becomes an
idyll, a consumable life feeling. And it is the
task of architecture to precisely encapsulate
this image, to be a presentation and projection
surface for the different makes that now
constitute the Volkswagen group: flexible and
international.

The pavilions scattered around the land-
scaped park are by no means urban. They look
more like Baroque summer residences; sophisticated impressions in the midst of a gigantic
playing field. Each makes its own appearance.

While the car manufacturer suffers due to its
own platform strategy, whereby the same technology is used in different makes such that
buyers sheer off towards the equally good, but
less expensive daughters Seat and Škoda, the
firm Henn Architekten from Munich designed
distinctly individual pavilions. Architectural
variety was their motto, like those designers for
major companies who fit the widely differing
shells over the same floor plan components. The
idea was to translate trademarks into tangible
architectural forms—Audi's rings inspired an
elliptical pavilion with a central ramp while the
Škoda pavilion plays with the idea of fairytale
worlds and all things Czech: "A Message from
a Small Country Beyond the Mountains" is the
title of the accompanying brochure. Meanwhile,
in the radial building, tons of lead crystal glitter
in an absurdly vivid counterbalance to the otherwise dominant technology.

Spanish Temperament

Seat on the other hand features Spanish
temperament and *joie de vivre*. As soon as
visitors reach the ramp, percussion is heard.
The rhythms swirl around until the visitor
steps across the threshold to the sound of
"Sssseat." Perhaps because the perforated
"S" logo of Seat doesn't necessarily suggest a
pavilion, the focus here is on natural symbols:
a snail and a leaf entwined in an amorphous
shape. What is only hinted at in the Škoda
pavilion is perfected at Seat: the sanctification
of the automobile. After progressing through a
whole series of vestibules, visitors are led down
into the heart of the pavilion. Laser lights greet
them, cool blue drips from the walls, and it
seems as though one has traveled thousands
of years back in time. In a modern hypogeum
Seat's design concept study emerges from a
circular opening in the floor: flowing forms and
pure aerodynamics, the automotive goddess
remains behind glass, unattainable—Sleeping
Beauty. At the other end of the spectrum,
Bentley sweeps the visitor away on a mystical

Beguiling colors by night: two of the glass multi-story car parks in Wolfsburg with the Volkswagen pavilion in the foreground.

journey; buried deep in the artificial hill, this most traditional of makes appears to be contained in a gigantic necropolis. The visitor spirals down into the earth, past pounding motors and video screens. The ensemble is so charged with symbolism that it seems the very walls are bursting and cracking. The form of the hill echoes the racetrack at Le Mans; green granite alludes to enduring market values. Volkswagen's "world forum of automobility" becomes an architectural hodgepodge, with symbolically overloaded representative structures. Passing through the long passages of the Company Forum, the visitor leaves a site that palpably strives to make its mark. It was supposed to become an automotive pantheon, but the real outcome is architectural pandemonium.

Wolfsburg puts its faith in grand architecture. Zaha Hadid is the architect of the science center, Phæno, and new attractions cannibalize the old. The pedestrian zone is lifeless, cold,

and run down, but change continues according to plan.

Wolfsburg is everywhere; the movement that can reshape perfectly ordinary towns as amusement and leisure complexes has just begun. What this will mean for social interaction, for daily life, and what it means to be part of an environment dedicated to commerce is as yet unclear. So far, daily life has repeatedly shown itself resistant to attempts to revamp squares and whole towns for the sake of purely commercial considerations.

1 "Stadt des KdF-Wagens" = "town of the Strength-through-Joy car." Even before the foundation stone of the car factory was laid on May 26, 1938, the architect Peter Koller, on the instructions of Albert Speer, had already started work on plans for a model town, but only a small part of the center and three housing schemes were finished by 1943, when building works came to an end.

$E = mc^2$

Entertainment = Masscompatibilty x Coolness^2

Dream worlds are in vogue the world over, to the extent that one wonders in amazement why they haven't appeared earlier. They largely owe their existence to a unique concurrence on the threshold of the twentieth century, when capital funds and entrepreneurship coincided with numerous technical revolutions in the wake of electrification. For centuries, pleasure and luxury had been the sole symbols of power, embodied in villas in the Alban Hills outside of Rome, garden pavilions, and masked balls. With the advent of Modernism —founded on consumption and mass production—anyone and everyone had access to pleasure grounds or amusement parks. And these were urgently required. Coney Island served as an escape for the urban working classes and expanded dramatically in the Roaring Twenties alongside the rising income of the new middle classes and pen pushers. While the Depression halted the rise in material well being, Coney Island continued to prosper; when times are tough, there is an even greater need for illusion—and it was increasingly possible to make those dreams reality using the latest technology. At the New York World's Fair of 1939, Norman Bel Geddes's exhibition pavilion, Futurama, catapulted his guests into a world of unlimited growth and boundless mobility—into a not too distant future, a dream world just behind the Plexiglas panes of the visitor walkways. Luxury and high standards of living were no longer morally reprehensible goals, and after the First World War, they became part of the American Dream, seen at its most extreme incarnation in amusement and leisure parks. At amusement parks, everyone could feel important—at least for a moment. And it is precisely this fascinating connection that accounts for the uninterrupted popularity of the amusement park with its architectural coulisses.

In our present post-industrial society, dream worlds have long since become the flagship attractions of a worldwide entertainment industry which now standardizes and exploits individual yearnings to the same extent that it capitalizes on tried and tested ideas. This may seem to its critics like Hollywood-style cultural imperialism, an attempt to usurp traditions and to replace them with readymade products that are as tractable as they are profitable, but that only partially explains their success. In fact, dream worlds arise from a collective need to escape—albeit momentarily—from the bewildering reality of everyday life.

Virtual realities and real dream worlds have never been closer to each other. Globally the games industry has a turnover of around 35 billion dollars—more than the movie industry. Computer Generated Images (CGI) crucially influence the look of blockbuster films, and the screen and console are merging to form an interactive dream machine. Arguably the best action movie of 2004, *The Incredibles*, was computer-generated. The sequel will soon follow in the form of a computer game. Boundaries are blurring.

A Society of Communication

Nowadays dream worlds often appear much more attractive than many of the places where people live. They promise a future and growth in an age of ever-decreasing possibilities. While occupants of certain French suburbs vented their frustration in late fall of 2005 in acts of excessive violence directed against the state's systems and its citizens, the takings at the ever-expanding Disneyland Resort Paris went up. And although there may seem to be some contradiction here, in reality the two factors are closely intertwined. Dream worlds reflect a post-industrial society based on communication, where the blanket availability of video mobile phones, wireless LAN, and GPS systems raise, for the first time, the possibility of tracking every citizen's movements. So dream worlds offer a welcome escape route. They present simple solutions to complex issues; niches where people can leave behind the workaday world for a dream industry whose members are paradoxically just as hard working, interconnected, and profit-oriented. The only difference being that, having purchased an entrance ticket, no one wants to look behind the scenes. Whereas the eighteenth-century man still recognized contemplation and humility as prime values, during the course of the twentieth century the mass compatible culture of distraction and consumption has become a global aim. Amusement parks and shopping centers function according to the same principles the world over. They are the children of a thoroughly secular society and celebrate the triumph of popular culture, epitomized in Las Vegas which probably constitutes the most sophisticated form of entertainment that money can buy today — glittering, fascinating, and so complex that it has long since become the stuff of movies, literature, and university seminars. Las Vegas demonstrates how popular and elite cultures mingle. Dream worlds of this kind have become the cultural paradigms of the twenty-first century, where public spaces are replaced by closed private worlds, where the environment and time itself have been dispensed with in scenarios that substitute rather than imitate reality.

In the mid-1930s, the American journalist James Rorty traveled the length and breadth of the USA and came to the conclusion that people's longing for a "dream culture" was barely affected by the Wall Street Crash and the global economic depression. On the contrary, dreams were all the more in demand and the economy reacted accordingly: Detroit with the production of mobility, Hollywood with the creation of dreams, and New York with high-spirited radio shows. Two generations later, the book *Dream Worlds* was published following a journey through the United States of America. It documents one man's search for the sediment of our entertainment culture. The old ideal city is dead; numerous companies have taken on its role. They detach segments of the still-relevant notion of a better life and offer these to the consumer as perfected enclaves: shopping malls in which every wish is fulfilled, amusement parks vying to offer the biggest attraction and the most excitement, or stream-lined settlements like Celebration in the guise of towns, but actually laid out as a pre-modern village with small-scale, comfortable neighborhoods as an antidote to the technology-dominated, cold world outside.

That attractions are consumed like ice cream and outstrip each other at a breakneck speed is also evident in Las Vegas. With every refurbishment and new construction the city rises even more resplendent from the supposed ashes, with yet another jewel in its crown, as in the new Wynn Las Vegas, which — by the time of its opening in spring 2005 — had become the most expensive hotel project the world has ever seen. The engines of entertainment, driven by the desire to constantly surpass the status quo, are running at full throttle. Now, all over the world, there exists the same "pursuit of happiness" promised by the American Revolution, which — in its commercialized manifestation as a global culture of consumption — demands ever more spectacular buildings and scenarios. As yet there are no signs whatsoever of this process coming to an end.

BIBLIOGRAPHY

Adams, Judith A. *The American Amusement Park Industry: A History of Technology and Thrills.* Boston, MA: Twayne, 1991.

Baudrillard, Jean. *America.* London: Verso, 1989.

Berman, John S. *Portraits of America: Coney Island.* New York: Barnes & Nobles, 2003.

Bittner, Regina, ed. *Urbane Paradiese: Zur Kulturgeschichte modernen Vergnügens.* Frankfurt/Main: Campus, 2001.

Blakely, Edward James, and Mary Gail Snyder. *Fortress America: Gated Communities in the United States.* Washington, D.C.: Brookings Institution Press, 1997.

Brandon, Pam. *One Day at Disney.* New York: Hyperion Books, 1999.

Charyn, Jerome. *Movieland: Hollywood and the Great American Dream Culture.* New York: G. P. Putnam's Sons, 1989.

Cohen, Lizabeth. *A Consumers' Republic: The Politics of Mass Consumption in Postwar America.* New York: Knopf, 2003.

Coates, Stephen, and Alex Setter, eds. *Impossible Worlds.* Basel: Birkhäuser, 2001.

Duany, Andres, Elizabeth Plater-Zyberk, and Jeff Speck. *Suburban Nation: The Rise of Sprawl and the Decline of the American Dream.* New York: North Point Press, 2000.

Dunlop, Beth. *Building a Dream: The Art of Disney Architecture.* New York: Harry N. Abrams, 1996.

Eaton, Ruth. *Ideal Cities: Utopianism and the (Un)Built Environment.* London: Thames & Hudson, 2002.

Frantz, Douglas, and Catherine Collins. *Celebration, U.S.A.: Living in Disney's Brave New Town.* New York: Henry Holt & Company, 1999.

Hayden, Dolores. *Building Suburbia: Green Fields and Urban Growth, 1820–2000.* New York: Pantheon Books, 2003.

Koenig, David. *Mouse Under Glass: Secrets of Disney Animation and Theme Parks.* Irvine, CA: Bonaventure Press, 1997.

Rem Koolhaas, *Delirious New York: A Retroactive Manifesto for Manhattan.* New York: Monacelli Press, 1994.

Kretschmer, Winfried. *Die Geschichte der Weltausstellung.* Frankfurt/Main: Campus, 2000.

Kruft, Hanno-Walter. *Städte in Utopia: Die Idealstadt vom 15. bis zum 18. Jahrhundert zwischen Staatsutopie und Wirklichkeit.* Munich: Beck, 1989.

Low, Setha. *Behind the Gates: Life, Security, and the Pursuit of Happiness in Fortress America.* New York: Routledge, 2003.

Low, Setha M., and Denise Lawrence-Zúñiga, eds. *The Anthropology of Space and Place: Locating Culture.* Malden, MA: Blackwell Publishers, 2003.

Lüdi, Heidi, and Toni Lüdi. *Movie Worlds: Production Design in Film,* with contributions by Kathinka Schreiber. Stuttgart: Edition Axel Menges, 2000.

Marling, Karal Ann, ed. *Designing Disney's Theme Parks: The Architecture of Reassurance.* Paris: Flammarion, 1997.

McKenzie, Evan. *Privatopia: Homeowner Associations and the Rise of Residential Private Government.* New Haven: Yale University Press, 1994.

Mitchell, William J. *City of Bits: Space, Place, and the Infobahn.* Cambridge, MA: MIT Press, 1995.

More, Thomas. *Utopia.* Edited by George M. Logan and Robert M. Adams. Cambridge Texts in the History of Political Thought. Cambridge: Cambridge University Press, 2003.

Postman, Neil. *Amusing Ourselves to Death: Public Discourse in the Age of Show Business.* New York: Penguin Books, 1985.

Ross, Andrew. *The Celebration Chronicles: Life, Liberty, and the Pursuit of Property Values in Disney's New Town.* New York: Ballantine Books, 1999.

BIOGRAPHIES

The Author

Munich-based journalist Oliver Herwig writes for
various newspapers in Germany and Switzerland,
and teaches design theory in Basel, Karlsruhe, and
Linz. In 1999, he was guest editor at *wallpaper**
magazine, and he has received numerous awards
including the Karl-Theodor-Vogel Prize in 2000 for
outstanding journalism in the field of technology
for a reportage on British Airways London Eye.

The Photographer

Florian Holzherr works as a freelance photographer
for art and architectural publications in Europe and
the USA. As James Turrell's official photographer, he
has been closely involved in the life's work of this
great American artist. His clients include Allmann
Sattler Wappner, DIA Art Foundation, The Chinati
Foundation, SOM, and Dietmar Tanterl. He lives in
Munich, Germany.

ACKNOWLEDGMENTS

Many thanks to

Alpa Kameras for the best travel camera ever made
Richard Baker
Kiki Bauer for helping us in NYC
Eugene Binder for his hospitality in NYC
Stefanie Bradie
Roger Duffy
Howard Elkus
Mary Hoadley
Debrah Hopkins for the Paolo Soleri contact
Peter Jepsen
Elisabeth Lowrey-Clapp
David Manfredi
Darrell Puffer
Christa Raschke for the travel arrangements
Angeli Sachs and Sandra Leitte for editing
Walther Smith
Paolo Soleri
Lindy Thorsen
Robert Venturi and Denise Scott Brown